T0128423

A
Journey
to
Joy

How to find joy in the midst of grief,
heartache, or tribulations.

JOY BUERKLE

WESTBOW
PRESS®
A DIVISION OF THOMAS NELSON
& ZONDERVAN

This book is a work of non-fiction. Unless otherwise noted, the author
and the publisher make no explicit guarantees as to the accuracy of
the information contained in this book and in some cases, names
of people and places have been altered to protect their privacy.

WestBow Press books may be ordered through booksellers or by contacting:

WestBow Press
A Division of Thomas Nelson & Zondervan
1663 Liberty Drive
Bloomington, IN 47403
www.westbowpress.com
844-714-3454

Because of the dynamic nature of the Internet, any web addresses or
links contained in this book may have changed since publication and
may no longer be valid. The views expressed in this work are solely those
of the author and do not necessarily reflect the views of the publisher,
and the publisher hereby disclaims any responsibility for them.

Any people depicted in stock imagery provided by Getty Images are
models, and such images are being used for illustrative purposes only.
Certain stock imagery © Getty Images.

ISBN: 978-1-6642-8183-7 (sc)
ISBN: 978-1-6642-8184-4 (hc)
ISBN: 978-1-6642-8182-0 (e)

Library of Congress Control Number: 2022919554

Print information available on the last page.

WestBow Press rev. date: 10/26/2022

Consider it pure joy, my brothers and sisters, whenever
you face trials of many kinds because you know
that the testing of your faith produces perseverance.
Let perseverance finish its work so that you may
be mature and complete, not lacking anything.

—James 1:2–4 (NIV)

SPECIAL THANKS

*J*esus and His Holy Spirit for leading me to write and
publish this book.
My husband, Ryan, for being my biggest
fan and supporter. I love you, Ryan.
God and Matt, for introducing me to my husband, Ryan.
My mother, Paula, for writing a book and
inspiring me to do the same.
My twin sister, Lori, for being with me through it all.
My precious nieces and nephews, for inspiring
me to be the best version of myself.
My mother-in-law, Lena, for a speaking life over us.
Rick and Megan, for loving us from afar.
Emily, for being such a cheerleader throughout my years.
Aunt Judy and Uncle Tony, for inspiring
me to live life "bigly."
Aunt Melody and Uncle Larry, for their love and support.
Ryan's extended family, for praying for him
throughout the years to find his wife.
Amber and David, for teaching me
about the power of our words.
Judy and Taylor, for treating me like family.
Amy, for leading a grief group in my
desperate time of need.
Ima, for praying over me and speaking life into my future.

Gizzel and Tina, for being my best friends
through the hills and valleys.
Sara for always showing up and being a consistent friend.
Jasmin, for helping me grow spiritually.
Pastor Tyler and Maria along with Pastor Randy
and Nancy, for teaching God's word every week
at The Garden Fellowship in Grand Prairie.
Pastor Suzanne, for being the most amazing prayer
warrior, intercessor, and worship leader.
Elizabeth, for being my rock and mentor
through my hardest days.
Barrett's Bears Ministry, for helping me
through my pregnancy losses.
Gateway Church, for leading me into salvation.

I love you all more than my words could ever express.
Thank you all for being part of my journey.

DEDICATION

$\mathcal{F}$irst and foremost, this book is dedicated to God as I glorify His goodness through the hard times. Second, this book is dedicated to *you*. Wherever you are on your walk with Jesus, this book is available to help you understand and recognize God's true character.

When I began experiencing tribulations as a child and as a young adult, I did not fully know God or God's character. Oftentimes, I was confused, angry, or upset at God. Now that I have grown spiritually, and I have a loving relationship with our heavenly Father, I am here to share the Good News of His grace and love for you!

This book is for anyone going through grief, heartache, challenges, or trials. We will all experience sufferings in this world. 1 Peter 4:12 (NLT) tells us: "Do not be surprised at the fiery trials you are going through, as if something strange were happening to you."

I hope this book will encourage you to see divine intervention through any challenges or tribulations you may be enduring and remember that 1 Peter 5:10 (NIV) says: "After you have suffered a little while, God will restore you and make you strong, firm, and steadfast."

TABLE OF CONTENTS

Introduction xv

1. On the Mountaintop 1
2. In the Valley.. 9
3. A New Normal 19
4. Why Is This Happening? 25
5. Heavenly vs. Worldly 33
6. Triggers..39
7. Moving Forward 45
8. Embracing Life.. 53
9. Cloud Nine...61
10. Deep Waters..73
11. People Pleasing... 85
12. Urgency 93
13. Suffering Well 97
14. The Power of Words 105
15. Choosing Joy 113
16. The Waiting 119
17. Is Satan Out to Get Me? 127
18. Protect Your Peace...131

19. Your Ministry..137
20. Report for Duty...143

Study Guide/Group Discussion.........................153

INTRODUCTION

*A*fter losing my long-term boyfriend, Richard, to a brain aneurysm when I was twenty-eight years old, I hit rock bottom. I wanted the ground to open up and swallow me. Not only was I grieving over the death of Richard, but I was grieving over the loss of my best friend and the future we had planned together. I was grieving over "what could have been." I grieved over the trips we didn't take and all the places we talked about traveling to. Instead of planning a wedding, I was planning a funeral. I grieved over the future I had planned in my mind.

That is why I wrote this book. No matter what we plan or what we think our life should look like, the Lord's plan will always prevail. "For I know the plans I have for you," declares the Lord, "plans to prosper you and not to harm you, plans to give you hope and a future" (Jeremiah 29:11 NIV).

If this book can help change one life, then my assignment of writing this book is fulfilled. I hope that one person is *you*. By the way, my name is Joy, and I'm really glad you're here. I know you've gone through some hard days. My healing began when I started sharing my story, so I hope this book will inspire you to share your story, too. This book is my journey to finding joy and my testimony of God's goodness. May God speak to you through this book as He continues to hold your hand on your journey.

Just like Jesus, "I show my scars so others know that they can heal, too."

The Bible tells us in Galatians 6:2 (NIV) to carry each other's burdens. Whatever you might be going through, I'm here for you, and I hope this book can help you. I pray that the Lord provides you with peace, comfort, and strength and surrounds you with an endless amount of love. I pray that there are more good days than bad days. Most of all, I pray that you will have the strength and courage to choose the gift of *joy.*

Love,

Joy

Joy: gladness not based on circumstance.

Chapter 1

ON THE MOUNTAINTOP

*A*s I entered adulthood, I was determined to climb the mountain that was before me. I didn't have a magical upbringing or a lot of happy childhood memories. As a child, I resented that I didn't have a father figure in my life. I was close to my fraternal twin sister as our mom dedicated most of her time and energy to working as much as possible since she was our family's only provider. We didn't have close family members, extended relatives, or inspiring mentors in our lives, so other than the schoolteacher we had each year, my sister and I practically had to raise ourselves.

When my mom wasn't working, she tried to take us to church every so often, and she was able to send us to a couple of church camps, but I didn't grow up truly *knowing* the Lord. I got baptized at age eight because I saw other kids at church getting baptized, and when I asked my mom about it, she scheduled my sister and me to get baptized the following week. I did not understand the true meaning of getting baptized, but I got baptized anyway. I did my best to read my Bible, say my occasional prayers, and hang out with the right people at school as I thought that was enough to consider myself a Christian. I didn't know how to have a personal relationship with our heavenly Father, and my childhood was filled with a lot of loneliness, sadness, and anger—not joy.

My mom worked in the health-care field, and she mostly chose the night shifts since that shift paid more money. We were a very low-income family that lived paycheck to paycheck and received some monthly help of Social Security and government aid. As I watched my mother pawn our TV or borrow money from friends to support us, I knew I did not want to experience that type of struggle and dependence on other people when I became an adult. It motivated me to become self-sufficient, independent, and successful.

My upbringing had very little structure and a lot of physical, emotional, verbal, and mental abuse. As a teenager, I stayed as busy as possible to hide and ignore the pain I felt from living in such a broken home. I began taking dance lessons at a dance studio and continued dancing for many years. A new passion developed, and I was able to use my dancing skill set toward joining the color guard "sport of the arts" team in ninth grade and I stayed on it throughout my high school years.

I continued to climb my mountain with dancing and color guard as I also became part of Winter Guard International

(WGI) for several years and was honored and humbled to win my high school talent show my senior year. My family did not have the opportunity to travel or take vacations. Still, I received the excitement and experience of flying in an airplane for the first time as my WGI team competed in the world championships in San Diego, California, during my junior year. All these experiences groomed me and set me up for personal independence and success.

After I graduated from high school, I continued with my passion for dance and color guard by participating in Drum Corps International. I traveled and competed with my team for three summers. This experience of being away from my house and hometown for three months at a time gave me a new sense of independence. Sometimes I missed my mom, but the organization kept me focused and busy. I didn't love living on a summer tour bus, but I valued and cherished the talented athletes I met along the way from all over the world. I also had the experience of a lifetime by touring and competing with my team in Europe while visiting London, Paris, Belgium, and the Netherlands. I was climbing that mountain and soaking it all up along the way!

I prayed to God now and then, but I was spiritually blind. It wasn't until later in life that I came across the scripture of Isaiah 42:16 (NIV), which says: "I will lead the blind by ways they have not known, along unfamiliar paths I will guide them; I will turn the darkness into light before them and make the rough places smooth. These are the things I will do; I will not forsake them." The Lord never left my side. He was always there guiding me, and I was oblivious to all the little gifts and miracles along the way. I wasn't giving Him the glory.

In the months I wasn't touring and competing, I was selling diamonds in a retail store in my hometown. This was my first "big girl" job! I wanted to work in this environment because I loved dressing up and wearing high heels. It made me feel professional, independent, and successful, which was the dream life I envisioned for myself as a young girl. I later realized that my mom's work ethic and determination were instilled in me.

I obtained my Diamond Counsel of America certificate and continued my love of dance and color guard as I taught junior high and high school teams. If you had met me during this time, you would have thought I came from an excellent family with a rosy life, as I got good at wearing the "happy mask." I wanted to control the perception of how others saw me, so I kept my childhood pain hidden while giving off a bubbly, fun, and sunny disposition.

When I turned twenty-one, I got the desire to move away from my hometown in Arkansas. I wanted to establish a new life, so I came to the great state of Texas. I moved here with a dear friend as I transferred to a new diamond store, and I joined a world-class WGI team in Dallas. This is where I made some lifelong friendships as I was climbing my mountain.

The first person I met in Texas was a man named Richard through the company for which I worked. I was drawn to his sweet smile and sense of humor. I also admired how he calmly and professionally managed difficult customers and stressful situations within our place of employment. He always looked dapper and had a professional demeanor. We remained acquaintances for three years while working within the same company. When I left to go to another company in the same industry, we lost touch for about a year.

Later, Richard reached out to me as he said he randomly thought of me that day. It was great to hear his voice and reconnect. We began talking on the phone, went on many dates, and spent a lot of quality time together in my town of Lewisville, Texas. We grew closer to one another, and I experienced falling in love and having a boyfriend for the first time at age twenty-four. I had a difficult time trusting men as I hadn't grown up with any male figures in my life, but Richard was different. He was soft, was kind, and always made me laugh. He treated me with immense honor and respect, and he had a caring and empathetic heart that I adored.

Richard and I continued to work hard in our careers, and I also began dancing for a competitive football team in Plano, Texas, where I was the dance captain. I left the diamond industry after six years and started a career as an admissions advisor at a local university. Amid our busy schedules, Richard and I took our first vacation together to San Francisco, California, during the summer month of July, which was our three-year anniversary. We continued to grow closer, and we loved talking about hopes and dreams for our future.

Looking back, I realize that if the devil can't make you bad, then he'll make you busy, and I sure was busy. I was busy climbing my mountain. The evil one had me in a wonderful place of busyness and contentment. I didn't see a true need for God. I believed God existed, but I didn't see a reason to call upon Him as I was already experiencing so much happiness. I was working, dancing, and traveling often to visit my family in Arkansas, which was a five-hour drive each way. I was young, vibrant, and in the best shape of my life. God did not have a place at the top of my priority list. He was further down my list as I would listen to Christian music in the car, but that was my definition of being a Christian. I didn't take the time to spend quality moments with Him. I didn't understand the reason.

The last month of my twenty-seventh year was when I reached the peak of my mountaintop! Richard and I were celebrating our four-year anniversary and began talking about the possibility of marriage. He also bought a dream home in Richardson, Texas! As he showed me the house for the first time, I walked inside, thinking, *This will be the house we will raise our future children in. This will be the home we will grow old in.* This home was so beautiful because it was full of hopes and dreams. Richard was so happy, and he kept saying, "Life is going to be so good!"

Perhaps that was God preparing my heart for my journey to joy.

Little did I know that this peak of my mountain was my last full month with Richard on this earth and all this beauty would soon vanish before my eyes.

Chapter 2

IN THE VALLEY

*W*ednesday, August 12, was the day my world turned upside down. Richard was rushed to the hospital by ambulance as he was unresponsive. Richard's mom and I drove to the hospital right away and nervously waited in the waiting room to hear from the doctor. His mom kept saying, "I don't have a good feeling about this ..." as I sat there shaking with anticipation to see Richard or hear from the doctor.

I'll never forget when the doctor walked into the waiting room and asked me, "Has Richard been having headaches?" My world shattered when she informed me that Richard had internal bleeding on his brain due to a ruptured brain aneurysm, and they needed to get him to the ICU at another hospital promptly. I stared at her with big eyes as I could not even process the information I had received. I had a moment to go back and see Richard before they had to quickly put him in the helicopter. They had him on the hospital bed, surrounded by several doctors and nurses. I noticed they had already shaved half of his head and began draining the blood from his brain. Richard's mom looked deeply into the doctor's eyes and loudly said, "You need to do whatever it takes to save my son! He is my only son!" We all stood there with tears, including the doctor with whom she was speaking to. The doctor said, "I can assure you that I will do everything possible."

They immediately care-flighted him to Dallas Methodist Hospital as they informed us that they had a room waiting for him in the Neuro ICU. It was early in the morning, and traveling from the town of Richardson to Dallas required transportation by helicopter so they could get him there as quickly as possible, considering the early-morning traffic.

I tearfully called my twin sister right away to inform her that something terrible was happening. I told her I was going to Dallas Methodist Hospital because Richard had a ruptured brain aneurysm. Knowing she was a strong Christian lady, I asked her to boldly pray with all her might. Neither of us could form sentences as we both cried, and then we hung up the phone.

Richard's mom and I watched the helicopter take off, and then she drove us to the hospital they were taking him to. I nervously sent a few text messages to some close friends, informing them of what was happening. As we got to the hospital and made it to the ICU, I noticed that my manager, Elizabeth, was already waiting for me. Just a month prior, I had left the university I was working at to go back into the diamond industry to work in one of Elizabeth's stores. She was my favorite manager in the diamond industry, and I was reunited with her after several years. Here she was, waiting for me at the hospital when I needed her the most. She had tears flowing down her face and told me that she saw Richard in his room and pointed to his room: Room 5201.

I slowly walked into his room, trying to grasp the concept that we were just having a bowl of ice cream together the night before, and now I'm seeing him in a hospital bed this morning, hooked up to machines, sedated, and with a ventilator down his throat. I could not understand how this was happening. The doctors informed me that he was in a coma and to keep talking and touching to a minimum. If overstimulated, his blood pressure would go up, and they were trying to keep that under control. At this point, they could not tell us about the prognosis until further testing, so they stayed focused on keeping him sedated and getting the blood drained from his brain.

Richard's family members started rushing to the hospital throughout the day. That evening the doctor pulled us all into a room to tell us the next steps of further testing. As I sat around Richard's family, I saw my sister walk by outside the window of our room. I began crying, not knowing that she got in the car right away and drove five hours to be with me. She left her three children and husband home in Arkansas as they were getting ready for the first day of school approaching, and my sister didn't know what Richard's outcome would be or how long she needed to stay in Dallas.

A dear friend brought me a journal to write in and told me to document all the visitors each day, along with writing down everything the doctor was telling me in case I forgot. I also added personal messages to Richard so I could give them to him when he woke up. The front of the journal said, *"For I know the plans I have for you, says the Lord."* I held tightly to that verse and began praying to God daily and every hour while writing down scriptures in the journal. The first scripture I wrote was, "Trust in the Lord with all your heart and lean not on your own understanding" (Proverbs 3:5 NIV). I also wrote down a personal message saying, "The moment Richard opens his eyes will be the best moment of my entire life. I am here waiting patiently with a heavy but hopeful heart."

I did not know the ins and outs of the Bible, but I was able to cherry-pick some scriptures to meditate on. I also saved scriptures that friends had texted me to get me through those dark days and unknown nights. This was the valley. I was in the valley. I was no longer at the top of the mountain, nor did I even care about the mountain or anything else that was happening in the world. Everything else around me seemed so small. I remained hopeful for Richard's outcome and grateful that he was in proper care. The doctor kept reminding us of how blessed Richard was to have made it to the hospital in a timely manner, as most people die instantly from ruptured brain aneurysms. I kept telling myself that Richard would make it through this because God must have spared his life for a reason.

After several days, the doctor told me I could start talking to Richard more. As I would speak to him, he would slightly move his limbs, which was a good sign. The nurse said my voice gave Richard a "calming effect." As I would talk to him, his eyelashes would get watery, and he would slowly turn his head toward me. He would try to move his mouth with the ventilator down his throat. I knew he could hear me because he would stop moving his mouth when I told him he didn't have to try to respond. Richard wouldn't open his eyes or respond to the doctor's commands.

August 17 was my twenty-eighth birthday. It was my best birthday up to that year because I got to spend another day on earth with Richard. I was at peace with however long his recovery would take. I didn't care how long the road would be; I was ready to walk it with him every step of the way.

Richard spent the next eleven days in the Neuro ICU as family and friends came in and out to show support with flowers, cards, and visits. I spent all my time by Richard's side or visiting with our loved ones in the waiting room or outside when I needed some fresh air. The previous November, I had rejoined my World Class winter guard team after several years of not performing with them. I thought I was retired from winter guard, but something in my soul told me to go back and do one last season. It was the best season of the team's history as we made it into the finals at World Championships. I was reunited with old friends, and months after the winter guard season had ended, those friends spent hours and days with me by my side in the hospital.

I was going days without eating or showering as I slept every night on the couch provided for me at the hospital. The sofa was beside Richard's hospital bed in his ICU room, and I wanted to stay near him if he woke up. After about seven days without a shower, a good friend insisted that I go home to get a good night's rest in my bed and to take a shower. She was unequivocal that I needed a shower. It was hard leaving Richard for a night, but I knew I needed to get some rest and take care of myself. I had nothing with me at the hospital, and I wore the same clothes daily. As I drove home, a song called "Same Power" by Jeremy Camp came on the radio, and it was the first time a song hit me in my soul. I began crying and screaming out to God to save Richard's life.

I returned to the hospital the following day to learn that things were taking a turn for the worst. Richard's breathing became very shallow, and they had him upright to drain his lungs as they informed me that he had developed pneumonia from being immobile for over a week. After a few more days, the doctor told all of us there that Richard had a slim chance of making it through as the days were approaching to begin considering taking him off life support. I didn't understand, and I screamed out at the top of my lungs. I cried while closing my eyes tightly and shaking my head, saying, "I'm not ready, I'm not ready …"

I did not know what to do, and I didn't want to be around anyone, so I went to the chapel on the bottom floor of the hospital and got on my knees and prayed the hardest I had ever prayed. This was the first time I had ever prayed on my knees. I had never needed God until God was the only hope I had. I had complete faith that Richard would pull through, and I believed it with every ounce of my being. I needed a miracle, and I was begging God and crying out for it. I now knew the true meaning of faith, hope, and love because it was all I had left.

The morning of Sunday, August 23, was when the doctor came in and woke me up before the sun was up to inform me that it was time for me to say goodbye. Richard's heart rate was slowing down, and he didn't have much time left. I remember staring at the doctor, still half-asleep, thinking, *this is a dream … this isn't happening.*

My twin sister was in the room with me, and I'll never forget the angelic look in my sister's eyes as she placed her hand on Richard's leg and calmly said, "This is good; you don't have to decide to take him off life support. He's going home on his own … let him go home." She then stepped out of the room to give me time alone with Richard as she began making phone calls to the family.

An overwhelming sense of peace came over me. I had never felt God's grace and presence more than I felt at that moment. I spent about thirty minutes by Richard's side as he left this earth. As soon as his heart rate stopped, and the machine flat-lined, I wrapped my arms around him, laid my head on his chest, and sobbed. After a while, the doctors had me leave the room so they could remove the ventilator and all the cords that were attached to the machines. I said one last goodbye to Richard, and then my sister drove me home.

I'll never forget coming home and how difficult it was for me to walk up the stairs. I got into the shower, barely able to move my body. I was in so much emotional pain and disbelief. I was also physically and mentally exhausted as I hadn't slept much or eaten food in eleven days. Many friends came over that day, and then I was finally able to crawl into my bed late that night. I laid there ... in the valley ... desperately needing God. I began crying out to a God that I was genuinely meeting for the first time.

That night before I fell asleep, I wrote in my journal:

> "Early this morning, I had to say goodbye to the love of my life. Richard went home peacefully in my arms as I hugged him, kissed him, and told him everything would be okay.
> Richard, you are healed. You lived a good life. You fought a good fight. I am so proud of you. You impacted so many lives. You taught me how to love ... unconditionally. You have nothing to worry about. You are home, and I will see you again someday.
> I love you with my entire heart and soul."

Blessed are those who mourn,
for they will be comforted.

—(Matthew 5:4 NIV)

Chapter 3

A NEW NORMAL

The rug was pulled out from under me, and I had no choice but to find a new sense of "normal" as I went through the days of grieving. I began planning Richard's funeral arrangements with his family, so I put my grief and mourning aside to try to give Richard a memorial service that he greatly deserved. I was busy planning a balloon release memorial and renting white chairs for the funeral that was held inside the home he recently bought. My heart drops as I think about the house that he just purchased becoming a place where we would all gather to honor his life.

People came to visit me daily, which was a true gift and a great distraction. I was continuously hearing that I was "so strong," but people didn't see how hard I was crying behind closed doors. I was just trying to survive and get through each day. I didn't have any other choice. I was simply going through the motions of each day as I lost a sense of the days and hours. I realized that when you're deeply grieving, you began to lose a sense of "time."

Friends and family traveled in from all over the nation, and the day had approached to honor a life that ended too soon. I knew I wanted to get up and speak at his funeral, but I couldn't find the words or the strength to prepare anything. Hours before his service, I wrote down some thoughts on two pieces of paper and ripped them out of a spiral notebook to have handy during the funeral. I had tears streaming down my face and the papers were shaking in my hands. I didn't want to live with the regret of not speaking at his service, so I got up, went to the front, and said these words after thanking everyone for the visits and gifts:

> "Thank you, Richard, for choosing me to spend your last four years with. One thing that brings me peace is knowing you left this world so happy … the happiest you had ever been. There was never a day that went by without constant laughter. An argument never lasted long, because one of us would always crack a smile. I will miss all our inside jokes. The jokes that no one will ever understand, but that's what made them so special. One thing I love about you is how you were able to relate to anyone. You always saw the good in everyone and I admire how you lived your life with open arms. Always accepting and encouraging others.

Although it doesn't seem fair, I know you had to leave because your body had served its purpose, your soul had done what it came to do, learn what it came to learn, and then you were set free. As you were leaving, a sense of calmness came over me because I knew you were going somewhere spectacular.

Getting to hold your hand, talk to you, and kiss you as you went home has been the most beautiful moment of my life. Thank you for choosing me to share that with. I find my strength by thinking about what type of encouragement you would give me through this time. Thank you for teaching me how to live life one day at a time. You taught me how to live life to the fullest, but most of all, you taught me how to love. I never knew there was such love inside of me.

Richard, you are healed. You lived a great life, you fought a good fight, and I am so proud of you. I can't wait to see you again."

As I went through the days and weeks following Richard's death, I began thinking about God and Heaven more than ever before. If that's where Richard was, then I wanted to be as close to him as possible. I tried reading the Bible as a young teenager, but I never made it past Matthew, Mark, Luke, and John; the first four books of the New Testament. I had so many questions about faith and eternity, so I began asking God. As I would talk to God, I would start to have doubts, and I would question, "Is all of this even real?"

I started to question whether Jesus was indeed the Messiah ... or was he just a man? One night following my doubtful days, I had a vivid dream with a loud audible voice that said to me, *"Jesus is the only way to Heaven. You have to believe. He is real."* I remember that dream so clearly, and from that moment forward, there was no turning back for me. The Lord came after His lost sheep, and I had been shaken and moved by the Holy Spirit. We are told in Acts 1:8 (NIV) that we will receive power when the Holy Spirit comes upon us, and Deuteronomy 5:25 (NIV) says: "The Lord our God has shown us His glory and His majesty, and we have heard his voice from the fire." During my deep grief, I heard the Lord's voice. I began to study and learn how God spoke to a lot of people in dreams in the Old Testament, so I didn't want to chalk up my dream as a coincidence or push it aside.

I was on the mountaintop for the first ten years of my adulthood, but I didn't experience true joy until I fell into the valley. However, the joy didn't come instantly. In the midst of heartache, I had to search for joy and choose it through the power of the Holy Spirit. Psalm 126:5 (NIV) teaches us that those who sow with tears will reap with songs of joy.

I began praying and reading God's word more than ever before. I prayed for God to heal Richard during those dark hospital days, but now God was revealing to me that I was the one He was healing all along. Jeremiah 33:6 (KJB) says: "Behold, I will bring health and cure and I will reveal the abundance of peace and truth." The Lord was doing a work in me and saving my life. I was talking to God more than ever, and each day of my grief journey was pulling me closer to

Him. Matthew 11:28 (NIV) says: "Come to me, all you who are weary and burdened, and I will give you rest."

There were some extremely hard days on my grief journey such as donating Richard's clothes, helping his mom clean out and sell his house, and revisiting old photos and voice messages. In some moments I felt strong in the Lord and other moments I felt as though my heart had been ripped out of my chest. Most of my pain was realizing that the world was still turning although my world had stopped. I prayed every day for God's peace and comfort.

I continued trusting and hoping in God and prayed without ceasing. Psalm 13:5–6 (NLT) says: "But I trust in Your unfailing love. I will rejoice because You have rescued me. I will sing to the Lord because He is good to me." I was fasting and meditating on God's word daily. This was my new normal. I had a new "comfort companion" in Christ Jesus. "Knowledge" is something that we "study" or something that we "experience," and I was truly experiencing the Lord before I ever began reading His word. I knew Jesus through the comfort He was giving me before I learned more about Him. I was spiritually hungry to know more about this amazing God that was embracing me with so much love, comfort, and guidance during the darkest days of my life.

This was my new "normal." I began experiencing unexplainable joy in the midst of deep grief.

The joy of the Lord is my strength.

—Nehemiah 8:10 NIV

Chapter 4

WHY IS THIS HAPPENING?

*W*hatever you have gone through or whatever trial you are currently facing, it is human nature for us to ask, "Why?" "Why is this happening?" When we go through hard times, that is the infamous question we all seem to have. We all want that quick answer to "why?"

Oftentimes, we may even be quick to blame God for the terrible things we are enduring. Problems force us to look to God, but God does not cause bad things to happen. We are told in Jeremiah 29:11 (NLT): "His plans for us are good and not for disaster. To give us a future and a hope."

God doesn't even like to destroy the wicked as He tells us in Ezekiel 33:11 (NIV): "I take no pleasure in the death of the wicked, but rather that they turn from their ways and live." James 1:13 (NIV) also says: "When tempted, no one should say, 'God is tempting me.' For God cannot be tempted by evil, nor does he tempt anyone."

Our world is made up of good and bad, and we also have the beautiful gift of free will, which is the power to choose between doing good or evil. Without the bad, we would not know what goodness is. Without sorrow, we would not know what true joy is. Jesus warned us in John 16:33 (NLT) that here on earth we will have *many* trials and sorrows. However, He reassures us in 1 Corinthians 10:13 (NIV) that He is faithful, and He will not let us be tempted beyond what we can bear. He also says that He'll be there for us to provide a way out so that we can endure it.

I began learning that we will never be completely happy on this earth because we're not supposed to be. It's not our permanent home. We will have happy moments, but it's nothing compared to what God has planned for us in Heaven. Each trial draws us closer to God. Each problem grooms us to be more like Jesus. Life is very brief compared to eternity, and we won't be here long, so we can't get too attached. The Bible explains that life on earth is like living in a foreign country. Earth is just our temporary assignment; it's not the end of the story.

2 Corinthians 7:11 in The Message Bible says: "Isn't it wonderful all the ways in which distress has brought you closer to God? You are more alive, more concerned, more sensitive, more human, more passionate, and more responsible."

When sad things happen, the good news is that God specializes in working everything out for us if we will call upon Him. God will use our situations to teach us perseverance and to build our character, which prepares us for Heaven. *Circumstances* are temporary, but *character* is forever. Genesis 50:20 (NIV) says: "You intended to harm me, but God intended it all for good."

It may take some time to realize "why," but Jesus tells us in John 13:7 (NLT): "You don't understand now what I am doing, but someday you will." No matter how painful it is now, someday you will look back and see that the struggles changed your life for the better.

After Richard passed away, someone said to me, "I don't understand why this happened to you, but what you're going through makes me want to run home and tell my husband how much I love him." At that moment, I realized that God could use my heartache and my tragedy to change someone else's view on life, love, or eternity. I quickly discovered that God was using my devastating experience so that He could help change the hearts of others.

When Richard was no longer here on earth with me, I surrendered everything to the Lord. I put all my trust in Him and matured spiritually while growing deeper in my faith. Isaiah 40:31 (NLT) tells us: "Those who trust in the Lord will find *new* strength. They will soar high on wings like eagles. They will run and not grow weary. They will walk and not faint."

Where I am now in my life as I draft this book is a true testimony of Romans 8:28 (NIV), which says: "And we know that in all things God works for the *good* of those who love Him." Not "some things" not "most things," but *all* things.

All we must do is love God! I would not trade my journey for anything because it led to something so good.

Years after experiencing the great tragedy of losing a loved one, the Lord blessed me immensely. The Lord restored Job, and He is going to do it for you, too. Job 42:10 (NIV) says: "After Job prayed for his friends, the Lord restored his fortunes and gave him twice as much as before!" I love that keyword, "*after* ... after Job prayed for his friends." As you reflect on that verse, who are some people in your life that you can pray for and bless even through your challenging season?

The enemy will try to give you thoughts that you did something wrong in your life to deserve the difficult things that you have gone through or the trials you are currently experiencing. It reminds me of John 9:2–3 (NLT) when Jesus' disciples passed by a blind man, and they asked Him, "Rabbi, why was this man born blind? Was it because of his own sin or his parent's sins that caused him to be blind?" Jesus said, "It was not sin that caused this. This man was born blind so the work of God can be displayed."

That story is such a reminder that God will use certain people to change the hearts of others, so other people can see His good works. If we can display God's goodness even through our challenging times, then others may come to Christ by witnessing our journey and our faithfulness. We may be the only Christian that some people meet, and they are watching us. They are observing us to see how we handle hard situations.

What you are going through can be a teaching moment for others. God has taken your pain and has entrusted you with an assignment because He knows you will fulfill it. He is calling on you to be a witness and to share your testimony of His love and His grace through the difficult seasons. Matthew 5:14 (NIV) says that you are the light of the world. (Yes, you!) Just like a city on a hilltop that cannot be hidden, in the same way let your light shine before others, so they will see your good deeds and glorify our Father in Heaven!

You are called to be God's light in this dark world, even through your tough times. Even through the darkest days, He just needs you to be an obedient and willing vessel.

In Hebrews 5:8–10 (NIV), we discover that Jesus relates to us as He learned obedience through the things He suffered. He tells us in James 1:2–4 (NIV) to "Consider it pure joy whenever we face trials of many kinds, because the testing of our faith produces perseverance and we must allow perseverance to finish its work so that we are mature and complete, not lacking anything!" That means that God will use those challenging situations to build our character! He also tells us in James 1:12 (NIV): "We will be blessed when we persevere under trial." So, this is your reminder to keep pressing forward. Keep shining your light. Keep going, keep walking, and keep searching for joy on the journey!

You are allowed to ask God "why?" but have patience because God, who began the good work within you, will continue His work until it's finished as we are told in Philippians 1:6 (NLT).

> Trust in the Lord with all your heart and
> do not lean on your own understanding.
> (Proverbs 3:5 NIV).

Dear Jesus,

No matter what the world throws at me, it is because of You that I can experience true joy. Sometimes it can be hard to be joyful amid adversity, but Your comfort gives me renewed hope and cheer. So today, I choose to rejoice because in Your presence is fullness of joy. No matter what I face, I will choose to joyfully worship You.

In Jesus' Name,
Amen.

Chapter 5

HEAVENLY VS. WORLDLY

I experienced deep grief after Richard passed away. That grief and mourning taught me so many valuable lessons. I had to let go of the person I loved more than anyone in the world at that time. "Grief is the price we pay for love." Richard gave me a love that some people search their entire lifetime for, and although our time together was limited, I am forever thankful for that gift from above.

It took me a long time to understand why God spared Richard's life as he spent eleven days in a coma, but when I'm silent and still, I hear the Lord say to me, "That was a gift to you, a time to say goodbye."

A life-changing lesson on my new journey of grief was learning how to surrender. The most selfless thing I could do was surrender. But what does that mean? "Surrender?" On the day Richard died, the Lord said to me in a Sarah Young's devotional, "Entrust your loved ones to me; release them into My protective care. They are much safer with Me than in your clinging hands." I was heartbroken because I wanted Richard to be here on earth with me, but I learned how to surrender by accepting that Richard did not belong to me. He belongs to our heavenly Father, and I had to surrender. Sometimes we are afraid to surrender because we don't want to lose control, but the truth is, we never had control; all we had was anxiety.

My biggest lesson was learning how to take Richard down from that pedestal to allow God onto that pedestal. Anything that we love more than God becomes an idol in our lives. Are there things in your life that you are making a priority over God? Is there something or someone that you need to remove from the pedestal to allow that seat for God? As much as Richard and I loved one another, it pales in comparison to God's love for us.

I learned more after Richard's death than I could have ever learned with him here on earth with me. His death left me with a beautiful gift—a new way of seeing. Life is not about the things we have, the car we drive, or the house we live. Life is about memories, laughter, and love, and the relationships we make along the way. That is the only thing we can take with us to Heaven. That lesson is usually learned by those who have deeply grieved or those who are dying. It's a lesson I wish I could give every living person because it would change the world.

Matthew 6:19 (NLT) tells us: "Do not store up treasures on earth but store up treasures in Heaven."

What are things you can do today that will impact the

kingdom? Our time here on earth as "temporary residents" is so fragile and so precious. The human experience that God gave to us is a temporary assignment when we look at the big picture. Our life is a vapor. James 4:14 (NLT) boldly says: "How do you know what your life will be like tomorrow? Your life is like the morning fog—it's here for a little while, and then it's gone."

Whatever you may be going through, I want to encourage you to live life "one day at a time," as we are not promised tomorrow. Eventually, (if it's in God's will), "one day at a time" will add up to a whole lot of days, and you'll be able to give God the glory for how far you've come. You'll be able to rejoice and celebrate the journey and the wisdom you picked up along the way. When we live one day at a time, it keeps us close to God and allows us to keep trusting and depending on God every single day.

We are told in Colossians 3:2–5 (NIV) to set our minds on things above, not on earthly things. This verse has also taught me that if the world were perfect, then we would never long for Heaven. What a beautiful longing the Lord has given us.

Someone once told me, "It's not how long we live, it's *how* we live." I am grateful for the heartache and the lessons throughout life's journey. I'm thankful for the gift of heavenly wisdom through the trials and for knowing God on a deeper level. It may take you a while to get to that place of thanksgiving, and if so, I pray that in the meantime you'll be able to carry your pain with a smile of gratitude knowing that the Lord, your God, is at work and *He will turn your mourning into joyful dancing!* (Psalm 30:11 NLT). Highlight that reminder in your Bible!

Did you know that Heaven is so much closer than we think? And God is already there preparing a place for us! He tells us in John 14:3 (NLT) that He is there, and when everything is ready, He will come to get us so we can be with Him where He is.

Sarah Young tells us in one of her devotionals that God is not limited by time or space; His Presence with us is a forever promise. We don't have to fear the future, for He is already there! Our future is already in His hands, and he releases it to us day by day, moment by moment.

Matthew 6:34 (NLT) reminds us to not worry about tomorrow, for tomorrow will bring its own worries. Today's trouble is enough for today. He also tells us in Matthew 6:27 (NIV) that we cannot add a single hour to our life by worrying. We have no reason to worry because He commands us in Joshua 1:9 (NIV) to be strong and courageous and to not be afraid or discouraged because He is with us wherever we go.

A moment of reflection: Are there materialistic things that are taking priority over your heavenly treasure? Are there earthly possessions that you need to let go of that are weighing down your soul?

"If we look at the world, we will
be depressed, but if we look to
God, we will have rest."

Chapter 6

TRIGGERS

After Richard's passing, I would tremble at the sight or sound of a helicopter. It would immediately bring me immense sadness. When the doctors discovered that Richard had a ruptured brain aneurysm, he was rushed to Dallas Methodist Hospital by a helicopter. His room was on the top floor in the Neuro ICU where the helicopters landed. As he spent eleven days in a coma, I stayed by his side, and I heard the helicopters land daily. The loudness of the propellers would make my heart sink.

My way of overcoming my helicopter trigger was by taking my nieces and nephew on a helicopter tour six months after Richard's passing. We were on a family trip in Gulf Shores, Alabama, and I wanted to associate a helicopter with a new memory—a positive one.

When triggers come over you, try to take a moment to pause and ask yourself some of these questions:

1. Can I slow down my breathing?
2. Who is in control right now?
3. What choice can I make?
4. Do I need to be alone?
5. Can I slow down my response?
6. What are my beliefs?
7. How can I take care of myself right now?
8. Will I regret the words I use?
9. How can I set a boundary?
10. Can I seek help or support?

The enemy will try to remind us of our pain and our past tribulations with "triggers." Triggers are things that remind us of the person we lost or the traumatic event we experienced. Triggers can also be holidays, birthdays, anniversaries, a song or a smell, or anything that takes us back to that place of sorrow. The beautiful thing is that we have the power over ourselves to choose how we will respond to those triggers. However, it is especially challenging when those triggers put us in "fight, flight, or freeze" mode, which is our brain's way of telling us that a problem or a threat exists. When we go into "fight, flight, or freeze," we experience that God-given adrenaline rush to protect ourselves. This is the same type of adrenaline rush that happens if we were to see a bear in the woods, but our brains cannot differentiate between a bear in the woods or a traumatic reminder, therefore, we go into "fight, flight, or freeze."

If you have triggers that attack you, I am here to encourage you to reframe that thought with something that brings you joy at that moment. The first step is getting your body and your brain out of "fight, flight, or freeze" and back into "rest and digest." One way to do that is to close your eyes while taking slow, deep breaths and then begin reframing your thoughts at that moment. Cognitive Behavioral Therapy teaches this, and it is also biblical! Philippians 4:8 (NLT) says: "Dear brothers and sisters, fix your thoughts on what is true, and honorable, and right, and pure, and lovely, and admirable. Think about things that are excellent and worthy of praise!" And Romans: 12:2 (NLT) says: "Don't copy the behavior and customs of this world, but let God transform you into a new person by changing the way you think." It is easier said than done, but the more you turn to God and His word, the more it will become second nature for you to allow Him to help you reframe your thoughts. When you train yourself to look for the blessings, you find them.

The Bible tells us to "be still and know He is God." I did not know what this verse meant until I experienced painful triggers. Sometimes we must be still in the presence of our heavenly Father and allow the world to move around us.

The main thing that helps me in those trigger moments is to memorize Bible verses and speak them aloud, such as, "The Spirit of God does not give us a spirit of fear, but of power, love, and a sound mind." (2 Timothy 1:7 NLT).

Speaking scriptures aloud has become my favorite way to rebuke the enemy amid triggers. Ephesians 6:17 (NIV) says:

"The sword of the Spirit is the WORD OF GOD." God's word spoken aloud is our greatest weapon against the enemy.

If you don't have Bible verses memorized yet, then you can start by expressing abundant gratitude to our heavenly Father when you feel triggers come upon you. Philippians 4:6 (NIV) tells us to "thank God for all that He's done and the peace of God, which transcends all understanding, will guard your hearts and your minds in Christ Jesus."

Jesus is the "Prince of Peace," and He wants to surround us with His love and peace. It's okay to feel sad as He grieves with us, and He is close to the brokenhearted (Psalm 34:18 NIV), but He does not want our hearts to be troubled (John 14:1 NIV), and He wants to be our refuge and our place of safety (Psalms 91:2 NLT).

We don't want to ignore the pain we are feeling, but we also want to be aware that we do not allow the enemy to lead us into a place of despair.

Sometimes the pain doesn't come back to visit us until years later. A counselor once told me that oftentimes we can be so focused on moving forward that we "pack away our pain in boxes" and we put those boxes on a shelf. She taught me that we unintentionally do that because it doesn't "benefit our survival" to unpack those boxes; therefore, we start to ignore that we have those boxes stored away. Once we get to a place of safety, such as a new marriage, a new town, or we start to slow down in life, then we unknowingly begin to unpack those boxes. An example of unpacking those boxes of pain is unintentionally putting up barriers with people, having unusual outbursts of frustration, or avoiding certain people, places, or things. This is when we need to recognize that the root of the pain is coming back up to the surface, and we need to urgently run to our heavenly Father who is right there waiting for us with open arms.

Psalms 55:22 (NTL) tells us to "give our burdens to the Lord, and He will take care of us. He will not permit the godly to slip and fall." So, if you have pain that is resurfacing, then that is an indicator that you still have some boxes in storage to donate to the Lord. It is so much easier said than done, I know, but it is too heavy, and it is not yours to carry.

Father, we lift up Your name. We are so grateful that Your truth drives away the spirit of fear and the lies of the enemy. We are safe under the wings of Your angels! You are good, and You have given us love, power, and a sound mind. Thank You, God.

In Jesus' Name,

Amen.

Chapter 7

MOVING FORWARD

To move forward, we must forgive and accept forgiveness to begin healing. I didn't fully realize what that meant until I read the story in the Bible about Jesus healing a paralyzed man in Mark 2:1–12 (NLT).

When Jesus saw the paralyzed man who was brought before him, he saw the man's faith and said, "My child, your sins are forgiven" before Jesus healed him externally. (Whoa! What?) God heals us from the inside out, and it starts with forgiveness.

The reason I mention the story of the paralyzed man in the book of Mark is because we may get impatient that we are not getting healed or moving forward as quickly as we would like. You may be asking God for miraculous healing and feel as though He's not listening.

It's a beautiful thing to get a miracle on the outside, but

it will never be better than the miracle of having our sins forgiven. The greatest miracle we receive is to have our sins forgiven. That is an unlimited gift to us—the gift that keeps on giving, a daily miracle.

Sometimes God is going to ask us to do something we've never done before, and we need to be bold enough in our faith to get up and walk. To move forward.

Perhaps you've experienced the opposite, where you are not ready to pick up your mat and walk. I experienced this type of resistance after losing Richard. I was afraid to move forward without him. My grief counselor told me that I was experiencing something called "survivor guilt." I felt guilty that I still had my life here on earth when Richard's life had ended. I went through a season where I didn't even want to eat because I didn't want to feel alive. Feeling alive made me feel guilty. Looking back, I realize that those feelings were not from God. God wants to restore us, and He wants to give us joy even amid our pain.

I learned that our most profound and intimate moments with God will likely be in our darkest days. I was reluctant to move forward because I had experienced our heavenly Father on a whole new level. I was afraid that I would let go of God's hand and not feel His closeness once I moved forward. It was as if I wanted the pain to stay with me because it brought me into the presence of Jesus. I would start to feel depressed that I was healing. Doesn't that sound so odd, like self-sabotage? I would have a vision that I wasn't clinging on to God's hand anymore. I was running ahead and looking back saying, "Look, Daddy, I'm running!" Then I had a vision that I ran so far away that I was lost in the woods. That vision taught me to not become so independent that I wouldn't need God anymore. God wants us to depend on Him. James 4:8 (NLT) says: "Come close to God, and God will come close to you."

God is always there waiting for us—just like the parable of the prodigal son. Jesus teaches us the story of the prodigal son in Luke 15:11–31 (NLT), which helps us understand the true character of our heavenly Father. No matter how far we drift away or how unworthy we feel to be His child, our heavenly Father is there waiting for us with open arms for when we return. He even wants to throw us a "welcome home party!" That parable helps us understand that God is a good and loving Father. He's not a tyrant; He's not a dictator. The Lord says in Isaiah 1:18 (ESV), "Come now, let us reason together." That is something that a good and loving Father says. He wants that relationship with us where we can go to Him, our heavenly Abba, and talk to Him about anything!

There may be days on your journey where you need to just "sit in the pain," and that makes sense as the only way to get through grief or tough times is to grieve. There may be days when your grief is so heavy that it's hard to get out of bed, but that sure makes the good days even more beautiful, and that's when we know what joy is. Joy is gladness that is not based on our circumstances.

As you endure the pain, you can have confidence knowing that there is wonderful glory ahead because God is at work on your behalf. He tells us in Isaiah 43:19 (NLT): "For I am about to do something new. See, I have already begun! Do you not see it? I will make a pathway through the wilderness. I will create rivers in the dry wasteland."

As I continued my grief journey, I put all my things in a storage unit as I did not have enough space in my new place. I decided that rather than living alone, I would rent a room from a wise, older lady that I met through a colleague of mine. That decision was the most humbling experience I had to face. All of mine and Richard's things packed away … the hopes and dreams of our future together … packed away. I felt as though I was on a ship that wrecked with everything floating around me. I went from being on a mountain top to starting all over again in the valley.

The room I rented gave me access to a bed, a small closet, and a dresser that all belonged to the owner of the house. So, all I took with me into my new home were a few bags of clothes to put in a closet and a dresser that did not belong to me. Over the course of a year, I continued to keep my things in a storage unit. I began slowly donating my things … but not "on purpose." I would encounter friends or coworkers that needed things such as a mattress or a TV stand, and I would give them what I had packed away. It began to feel liberating, so, I continued donating everything that I had until I no longer needed a place to store things. I'll never forget the last trip I made to my storage unit and how free my heart felt knowing that I was "letting go" of all my earthly possessions. Along with some sentimental things, I kept my suitcase, and I planned a trip to Ireland. I didn't feel "tied down" anymore; therefore, I had this new desire and urge to travel as much as I could. I felt free and liberated.

I traveled to Ireland, Gulf Shores, Cancun, and Las Vegas, and when I wasn't traveling, I was selling diamonds, selling travel memberships, and teaching a high school color guard team. I had a goal to save as much as I could to be able to make it on my own one day. I had a vision of buying a home in my name and proving to myself that I could do it as an independent woman.

It became difficult to want to set goals with moving forward because I became so close with the wonderful lady with whom I was living with. I did not have any family in Texas, and she became a "Texas Mom" to me. We would have coffee together every morning before the day took us in different directions. She was a listening ear and a shoulder I could cry on. When I would come home from a long day of selling diamonds, I was able to take off my coat of responsibility when I came into her home and lay my head to rest in my humble little room. I also loved that she had butterflies throughout her house. After Richard passed away, I would often encounter a yellow butterfly, which became my comfort from Heaven and my reminder that Richard was at peace.

The amazing lady that I lived with told me that I was also helping her. Thankfully, I didn't feel like a burden or an intruder since she had informed me that she encountered some financial struggles, and she would remind me that I was a gift to her as well by renting a room from her. I was also there to take care of her house, pets, and plants when she would travel to visit her family. It felt good knowing that I was a blessing to her, too. It's incredible when you can discover that you are helping the person who is helping you.

Sure enough, after two years of living frugally and renting a room, I was able to close on my very first home right before my thirtieth birthday. I also landed a corporate job that gave me better working hours, so I felt as though I was living the true American dream.

After two years of deep grief, I finally found new independence and excitement in life. While on my journey to joy, I began attending church regularly at Gateway Church in Frisco, Texas. I made the decision to rededicate my life to Christ, and I got water baptized as an adult on September 24. That day was also Richard's birthday, and the church happened to be doing church-wide baptisms that day. I knew that was the Lord telling me to rededicate my life to Him through baptism. The pastor asked me why I was getting baptized, and I said, "To give my life to Christ." I asked the Lord to take my life and use it for His glory. I said a prayer before getting baptized that those who don't know God will come to know God because they know me. Because Christ lives in me. (Galatians 2:20 NIV)

Richard's life brought me happiness, but his death led me to truly know Christ. I am grateful for the time I had with Richard, but I am more thankful that I was led into true salvation after his death. "For the kind of sorrow God wants us to experience leads us away from sin and results in salvation" (2 Corinthians 7:10 NLT).

Months passed, and I got so wrapped up in my new life that I started to lose that place of vulnerability and the real meaning of life. I wasn't praying as much or reading my Bible daily. I was dedicating my time and energy to my new job.

Perhaps my new career was taking a place on the pedestal where God was sitting the last two years of my life.

I loved the company I worked for until I realized that I was also selling something else—my soul. I was selling my soul to my career, and I missed my simple life. After two more years of my newfound independence and freedom, I took a leap of faith and resigned from my job. I knew there were probably a lot of people lined up waiting to take my position as the Lord told me it did not belong to me. I was not where He wanted me, and the Holy Spirit made that clear. After I boldly resigned, I took some time off from working and lived off my savings so I could "find myself" again.

One thing that filled my soul was traveling. So, I did some "solo soul traveling" to learn more about myself. I went to Florida, Washington, D.C., San Antonio, Colorado, and Los Angeles. I also went to San Diego with a wonderful friend, as well as a seven-day cruise to Cozumel, Belize, and Honduras. I was on a mission to find my soul again.

The time I had alone in stillness and in silence became a time where I could truly hear the Lord. I contemplated moving back to Arkansas to be near my twin sister and her family. At this point, I had lived in Texas for over a decade, so moving back to Arkansas was a big decision. I continued to pray for discernment and for the Lord to guide me into my next chapter. He kept telling me to "stay still" because He was working on my behalf. All I had to do was trust and wait for the door to open.

Chapter 8

EMBRACING LIFE

*A*s I began patiently waiting for the door to my next chapter to open, I realized that God had His hand of protection over me by putting certain people on my path all along the way. I was led into divine crossroads on my journey to joy. A lot of wonderful people came onto my path after Richard's passing. These people were new encounters, and they were people I would not have known if it weren't for Richard's death. I like to call these people "earthly angels." I met my "Texas Mom" through my coworker and that connection gave me a safe place to live for almost two years. Those things would not have happened for me if I did not go back into the diamond industry after my years of being an admissions advisor and met these new people in my life.

The house where I rented a room became a "healing place" for me and led me into a new season of growth. I also connected with the real estate agent that Richard used to buy his home, and that same agent is the one that helped me close on my first home. She was another one of my earthly angels. I was also recruited into digital marketing by the manager I had when I was an admissions advisor. All these people and experiences were grooming me for the next chapter on the journey.

During my waiting season of remaining obedient to where the Lord was going to lead me next, I stayed faithful in prayer. Romans 12:12 (NIV) tells us: "Be joyful in hope, patient in affliction, and faithful in prayer." I talked to God daily for discernment for my next steps as He tells us in James 1:5 (NIV): "If any of you lacks wisdom, you should ask God, who gives generously to all." I prayed that wherever the Lord led me that He would use me in a mighty way. Ephesians 2:10 (NIV) says: "For we are God's handiwork, created in Christ Jesus to do good works, which God prepared in advance for us to do."

Romans 8:18 (NLT) tells us: "What we suffer now is nothing compared to the glory He will reveal to us later." As I continued patiently waiting on the Lord, I reached out to a previous colleague I had worked with. She left the company a while before I did, and she was working for a smaller company within the same industry. She told me that she was loving the new company and that it was a blessing that I reached out. She continued, informing me that they had a position come open that day for which I would be a perfect fit. 2 Corinthians 5:17 (NIV) says: "Therefore, if anyone is in Christ, the new creation has come: The old has gone, the new is here!"

I sent in my resume, received a phone call, and then the next morning I was in Arlington, Texas, interviewing for the position. I remember sitting there in shock at how quickly this was happening. After interviewing for several hours, the CEO and the department director invited me out to lunch with some of the local employees. I signed the offer letter and agreed to start my new position the following Monday.

I lived north of the Dallas metroplex outside of Frisco, and this new position was in Arlington. With rush-hour traffic, I was commuting an hour and a half each way. I knew that I would have to decide to move closer, or I would need to request to work remotely from home. Philippians 4:6–7 (NIV) says: "Do not be anxious about anything, but in every situation, by prayer and petition, with thanksgiving, present your requests to God. And the peace of God, which transcends all understanding, will guard your hearts and your minds in Christ Jesus."

I was already in love with my new position two weeks in. The work I was doing was such a blessing and an answered prayer. This was my dream job, and I really valued and respected the company and its core values. John 14:18 (KJV) says: "I will not leave you comfortless: I will come to you." The Lord was providing for me, and I was truly thriving!

On the drive home after a long workday, I realized that

it would be much nicer to live closer to the office. I did not want to sit in the car for an hour and a half each way when I could use that time to get more work done. On my off weekends, I began looking at homes in the area to see what my options would be. I found some beautiful homes, but I knew that I would have to sell the house that I was living in, which was the first house I was able to call my own. I loved my two-story house with the beautiful balcony overlooking a park, but I didn't love the location as it required toll roads and a great deal of commuting. Realistically, my current home was too large for me. I often felt very lonely with the empty rooms and the tall ceilings, and I was excited to get something smaller to fit my needs as a single woman. I realized that a house is just a building, but a home is a feeling, and I didn't truly feel "at home." Psalm 37:4 (ESV) says: "Delight yourself in the Lord, and He will give you the desires of your heart."

As my new home search began, I found a couple of homes on which I was willing to make an offer. My free time was limited since I only had the weekends to go look at houses in person with my agent, so I was ready to make a decision quickly. I had a great relationship with my agent as this was the same real estate agent that helped Richard buy his home, and then she helped me get my first home. Now, here she was helping me again, and I was thrilled! Ephesians 3:20 (NLT) says: "Now all glory to God, who is able, through His mighty power at work within us, to accomplish infinitely more than we might ask or think."

I called my best friend one evening to let her know that

I was about to make an offer on one of two homes between which I was torn. I couldn't decide which one I liked the best, and I wanted her opinion. One of the homes was a two-story, brick house with a lot of space, which was similar to what I already had as far as the amount of space. The other house was an adorable one-story, yellow house in a similar type of neighborhood that I was currently living in for the last two years. As my friend looked at the two houses, she said, "Let me do some more research for you and see what else I can find."

Later that evening, my friend sent me a link to a house that was on the market in the same area where I was looking for a house. She said, "This house would be perfect for you." The house needed some cosmetic work as far as painting, but it was a perfect-sized one-story house that had three bedrooms, two bathrooms, and a front room that could be an office, a second living room, or a fourth bedroom. I also loved that the backyard had a deck, and it overlooked nature and a lake without any houses behind it. The home looked like an oasis, and it was only twenty minutes from my office, which was a much better commute. Revelation 21:5 (ESV) says: "Behold, I am making all things new."

This house was also newer and only had one previous owner, who kept the house in exceptionally good shape. I texted my agent, and she agreed to meet me the very next morning to look at it. As soon as I pulled up to the home, I loved the wide streets, the two trees in the front yard, and the beautiful front flower bed. We walked into the house, and it smelled like freshly baked cookies. As I walked around the house, I realized that this home had everything I needed. I also loved the open layout of the house and how the kitchen flowed nicely into the dining room and into the living room. I especially loved that this house did not have any stairs; my other house had the master bedroom upstairs.

I told my agent that I loved this home, and we moved forward with an offer on the house right away. Within days, we received the exciting news that my offer was accepted! I spent the next few weeks getting my current home packed up and ready for the market. I was eager to live closer to my new job, and the Lord was literally picking me up and moving me. Psalm 118:6 (ESV) says: "The Lord is on my side; I will not fear."

A couple of weeks prior to moving into my new home, I hired a painting company to paint the inside and outside of the house along with the cabinets in the kitchen and bathrooms. Within one month, I was already moving into my new place! I hired movers to move all my belongings including my boxes, furniture, and appliances. I also hired my repair person to remount all my TVs throughout the house in each bedroom, my two living rooms, and a small TV mounted outside on my back patio. It didn't take me long to get settled in, and I was so thankful to be in a new location that didn't require much commuting. I also loved that I picked a house just minutes away from Dallas and close to my office in Arlington. 1 John 5:14 (NIV) says: "This is the confidence we have in approaching God: that if we ask anything according to His will, He hears us."

It took me several months to sell my previous house, but I was grateful for my new career and my new home. I prayed for the Lord to use me in a mighty way, and He got to work and moved quickly. Philippians 2:13 (NLT) says: "God is working in you, giving you the desire and the power to do what pleases Him."

Chapter 9

CLOUD NINE

Several weeks into my new job, I got to know the company's president much better through casual small talk each time he would pass by my desk. One evening as I was getting off work, he said to me, "Joy, the more I get to know you, the more I want to introduce you to my buddy, Ryan." I was flattered, but I was very hesitant as I had just started this new career. I told him that it made me a little nervous because I wanted to do a really good job as a manager for this company, and I didn't want anything to get in the way of that.

He continued to tell me more about Ryan and how they grew up together and knew each other through church and Boy Scouts since they were ten years old. He also told me that Ryan was a pilot and that he had his own airplane and hangar. He showed me photos of Ryan, and I told him that those materialistic things didn't impress me because I knew what it was like to be on top of the mountain and then have the rug pulled out from under me. He told me that Ryan once told him that he would sell everything he had to have a family. My CEO asked if he could tell Ryan that he talked to me about him, and I told him that would be okay. He also told me that Ryan would be stopping by the office later that week, and he wanted to introduce me to him.

Several days later, Ryan came into the office, and as soon as I saw him, I remembered thinking that I could potentially be looking at my future husband. My CEO introduced me to him, which was very brief as I was very busy at work. My first impression of Ryan was that he was very humble, and I really admired that. I also noticed the cross around his neck, and his beautiful blonde hair and blue eyes, which I also admired.

Proverbs 3:6 (NLT) says: "Seek His will in all you do, and He will show you which path to take." About a month later, I proceeded to find Ryan on social media, and I sent him a friend request. Right away, he sent me a message and asked me out for coffee that following Sunday afternoon. I enjoyed getting some quality time to get to know Ryan better. He was such a gentleman by holding open the door for me, and I also appreciated how respectful he was by maintaining eye contact with me. He was a great conversationalist, and I felt very safe around him.

Ryan and I continued to go on lunch dates, dinner dates, and to the movies during the following weeks. He was exceedingly kind, generous, and gentle. Ryan always prayed over our meals and talked about his faith, and I loved that he was a man of God as that was so important to me. As I got to know Ryan more, I learned that his dad and his brother have the name "Richard." I felt as though that was a wink from God that I was on the right path.

I was having a slow time opening my heart to love again, so I had some barriers during the first few months of our dating life. I had also established new independence and contentment. Ryan remained so patient with me, and he never stopped pursuing me. I had spent the last four years grieving over Richard, and I was finally getting to a place of considering the possibility of a future relationship, and I had been praying over that.

It was a challenging transition starting a new career, buying a new home, and moving to a new town; but I remained obedient because I knew the Lord was answering so many prayers. I finally started to realize that all these recent changes I was going through led me to meet Ryan, which was God's biggest part of the plan. As I started to get more adjusted to my new career and my new home, I began going on more dates with Ryan and got to know him and his soul better.

Any time Ryan would come over to my house, he would discover ways to help me such as buying me a reusable champagne stopper, a laptop case, and dish soap. Those little acts of kindness really captured my attention and heart. I loved Ryan's attention to detail and his tender and generous heart.

That following October, Ryan asked me to be his girlfriend. It was a big surprise to my family and friends that I was in a relationship, and they were all so overjoyed for me as they continued to pray for me over the years. On our one-month anniversary of being in an official relationship, Ryan dropped by my house early in the morning and left me flowers and iced coffee on my doorstep. He went back home until I was ready to go out for brunch in Dallas to celebrate. He was slowly winning me over, and I was so appreciative of his care for me. Ryan would write me love letters and sing songs that he wrote me on the piano. Psalm 4:7 (NLT) says: "You have given me greater joy than those who have abundant harvests of grain and new wine."

I was falling deeply in love with Ryan more and more each day. Ryan took me to Memphis, Tennessee, to meet his mom and his extended family for the Thanksgiving holiday. On the way home from Tennessee, we stopped in Arkansas so Ryan could meet my twin sister and her husband along with their four children. It was a dream spending the holidays together, and I was truly on cloud nine. Ryan would remind me that he had prayed his whole life for me and that this was the time God had planned for us to meet. Not sooner, not later. He would tell me that God built him for me, to defend me from the mean things in this cruel world and to be my protector, my rock, my steadfast beacon in the darkness, to provide me unconditional love, and to be a forever friend. John 15:11 (NIV) says: "I have told you this so that my joy may be in you and that your joy may be complete."

We went to see my side of the family in Arkansas for Christmas, and Ryan also took me to Hot Springs, which was our very first romantic getaway together. We came back to Texas, and his family was here visiting, and I got the opportunity to know all of them better. I realized that I had something I never had before: getting to do things together, such as going to the ballet and traveling to visit family while making time for romantic moments such as horseback riding or getting a couple's massage.

Ryan was more than anything I had ever prayed for, and God was blessing us both beyond measure. Sometimes it would feel too good to be true, and Ryan would tell me that he was once living in a lonely, bleak dream before I came along, and now, he had been awakened to the opening scene of Heaven's full blessings for him. Ryan would thank me for trusting him with my heart, and he told me he would cherish it with white gloves and protect it with his life. The first gift he gave me was a beautiful heart necklace with pink diamonds. He told me he gave me this gift as a symbol of giving me his heart. I cried as I embraced all the blessings that were pouring down on me. Ryan was the product of my unanswered and answered prayers. I was experiencing a love beyond my imagination.

Genesis 2:18 (NLT) says: "It is not good for the man to be alone. I will make a helper who is just right for him." My journey led me to this place. All the pain, heartache, and tribulations led me here, and I was experiencing pure joy. I'm so grateful for the journey, and I wouldn't trade it for anything. The love Ryan and I have is worth all the pain I endured to get to this place. Richard now has a warm place in my memory; Ryan now has the full capacity of my heart. The ability to love again was a miraculous gift from God.

Ryan and I continued the journey of our dating season and enjoyed going on a romantic cruise and had such a wonderful time on the beach, snorkeling, and swimming with the dolphins. Several weeks after we returned home from our cruise, Ryan took me to a park with his guitar, and he proposed to me. I was so overjoyed that he asked me to be his wife after five months of being in a relationship. We were so ready to start our lives together. It was difficult being apart, and we couldn't wait to get married and move in together. Mark 10:9 (NIV) says: "Therefore what God has joined together, let no one separate."

A week after our engagement, the COVID pandemic hit, and we were all quarantined, and businesses were closed. I began working from home, which was an adjustment but a pleasant change for me. Ryan helped me set up an office at my house, and we would visit each other daily after work. This season of living in quarantine brought Ryan and I closer as we cooked many meals together, spent a lot of time at the park, and talked about the hopes and dreams of our wedding and moving in with one another once we were married.

Ryan's hope was that we could lease out both of the houses that we owned and purchase a new home together as a married couple. I told Ryan that I was feeling overwhelmed by the thought of moving again since I had just bought my home and got settled in. We decided that we would both purge things and rent out the house that he was currently living in for almost a decade. We concluded that it would be best to live in the house I had recently purchased rather than buy a bigger one. Looking back, I realize that the Lord brought me to this town and put me in a home to prepare it for my husband.

During our engagement season, we took romantic trips to New Orleans, Arkansas, and North Carolina. I also began planning our wedding during the pandemic, and we embraced our engagement months as we went shopping for a venue, cake, flowers, and additional wedding vendors such as photography, music, videography, and a coffee and wine bar. I also went privately shopping for my wedding dress, and it was a beautiful day when I said "yes to the dress" with my twin sister there with me on a FaceTime call.

Ryan and I had a beautiful engagement party at my home in June, which was also the one-year anniversary of the day we met. Later, we had a bridal brunch at my favorite restaurant in Plano surrounded by all our friends here in Texas. We found a beautiful wedding venue near our town and planned for an October wedding since October was the month that Ryan and I began our relationship.

A lot of people said that 2020 was the worst year of their life due to the pandemic, but 2020 was the best year of our life since that is the year we got engaged and married. I was so grateful that God worked through my CEO to lead me to Ryan. I never took that for granted, and I thanked God every day. I was realizing that I had been created for this moment; to become Ryan's wife. Romans 12:10 (NIV) says: "Be devoted to one another in love. Honor one another above yourselves."

Our wedding month had arrived, and we had family and friends travel in to be with us. It was so wonderful seeing our families as the pandemic had prevented more visits. My best friend had custom wedding masks made as we were among COVID. We had to reduce our wedding guest count from two hundred guests down to seventy-five guests, and we were at peace with that. I knew that a smaller, more intimate wedding with all our closest relatives and friends would make it more special and meaningful. 1 Corinthians 13:4 (NIV) says: "Love is patient, love is kind. It does not envy, it does not boast, it is not proud."

We had our wedding rehearsal the day before our wedding, early in the morning. We were so honored to have our entire wedding party there as we enjoyed being together and going out for brunch after the rehearsal. I spent that evening alone in prayer the night before our wedding. 1 John 4:19 (NIV) says: "We love because He first loved us."

Ryan and I wrote cards to each other to read on our wedding day. Ryan told me that he had prepared his entire life to make me his bride and that as he passes through his days, the mere thought of me brings tears of happiness to his eyes. He told me that if he could give me one gift, it would be for me to be able to see myself through his eyes, and only then would I be able to experience the vastness of his love for me. Ryan told me that I had created purpose in his life and that we were truly blessed by God's love and plan for us. It's mind-blowing how many events before us were just as God planned for us to exist, for us to be designed exactly how we should be—perfect for each other, now in this moment. Ryan told me that his arms are always open to me and that he is my protector and my provider, my rock in a hurricane, and that I would never be alone.

Today was the day we would commit to making each other our "forever." We were surrounded by people who truly love us. Not only our family, but friends that traveled a long way because they care, and they wanted to be there.

I told Ryan in my card to him that today was the day I get to marry the man of my dreams. Ryan has shown me what true love is. I felt so undeserving of this love, and it reminds me of God's love for us. Ryan set my feet on steady ground, and I told him that I was no longer "Joy," as I am now, "Joy and Ryan." I thanked Ryan in my card for his kindness, gentleness, love, effort, support, encouragement, soul, and his love for God. I thanked him for being my spiritual leader.

I walked down the aisle to the song "Heaven Knows," by Hillsong United. We had a beautiful ceremony with live music from Ryan's brother and our Gateway worship leader as they sang "The Prayer" by Andrea Bocelli and Celine Dion. Ryan's pastor that he grew up with was our ordained minister, and that was so very special to us as that was the same pastor that baptized Ryan as a young boy. We had a special Communion during our ceremony while our Gateway worship leader sang "The More I Seek You." After our beautiful ceremony, we took family photos and then entered the reception and danced to the song "Known," by Tauren Wells.

After our wedding reception, Ryan played the piano and sang to me, and then we danced to the song "We Dance," by Bethel Music and Stefany Frizzell Gretzinger, which our Gateway worship leader sang live. That night we went to a romantic bed and breakfast in Fort Worth and then went on a weeklong honeymoon to Key West, Florida.

Our wedding day was the most beautiful day of our lives as God ordained every moment of it. We did not want it to end. I told Ryan that if I ever wrote a book, it would be called, *A Journey to Joy*, and he said if he ever wrote a book, it would have the same title. We did not want to come down from cloud nine, and we haven't because our marriage lives every day here on cloud nine.

Chapter 10

DEEP WATERS

*F*ive weeks after our wedding, my husband and I received the exciting news that I was already pregnant. I took a drugstore pregnancy test at home, and I couldn't wait for my husband, Ryan, to come home so I could tell him the news! I put the pregnancy test inside our new marriage Bible as I scrambled for a quick and creative way to tell my husband that we were already expecting our first child.

Ryan came home from work and asked me about my day. I told him that I had been reading our Bible and that I marked a page for him to read. He opened the Bible to find the pregnancy test, and as he picked it up with wide eyes, he said, "That says pregnant!" I smiled and said, "We're having a baby!" We were both so happy, excited, and shocked that this was already happening for us!

The day arrived for me to have my very first ultrasound!

By this time, I was over eight weeks pregnant, and I had been waiting for this day—our baby's first photo! Ryan and I were so excited, surprised, and blessed with how quickly we conceived a baby. We got pregnant just weeks after our wedding, and we did not take this for granted. We know that some couples spend months or years trying to conceive as well as having to use medical interventions to help them.

Although we did not expect to get pregnant so quickly, we thanked God every day for the beautiful gift. On the day of my first ultrasound, Ryan drove me to my doctor's office as we were filled with excitement, joy, and anticipation. Whenever I felt nervousness, fear, or anxiety creep in, I would begin meditating on Isaiah 41:10 (NIV), which says: "Do not fear, for I am with you; do not be dismayed, for I am your God. I will strengthen you and help you; I will uphold you with my righteous hand."

Ryan walked me into the office of our ultrasound appointment, and as we walked up to the front desk to fill out paperwork, they informed Ryan that he could not go back with me due to COVID precautions during that time. As I walked back to the waiting room, I turned around to see my husband still standing there ensuring that I was safe. I sat there with nerves in my heart as I waited for the ultrasound technician to call me back. I had my phone ready as the front desk receptionist informed me that I would be able to FaceTime my husband as he waited for me in the truck. I sat there reading text messages of love and support from our family until the technician called me back.

I walked with the technician into the tiny ultrasound

room as I got my phone ready to FaceTime Ryan. I laid on the ultrasound table as the technician began the abdominal ultrasound. I was looking at the screen while occasionally glancing at Ryan's smile of excitement on my phone. The technician proceeded to inform and educate me about three fibroids she found in my uterus. She explained that they were noncancerous growths and that they are quite common, especially during pregnancy. She informed me that mine were small, and she did not seem concerned. The technician began explaining to me what she was seeing, such as my eight-week gestational sac along with the fibroids. She then told me that she could not find the baby and that she needed to bring in my doctor.

My doctor informed me that I was more than likely having a miscarriage as it appeared that my pregnancy had stopped progressing. She told Ryan and I that she wanted us to come back a week later to see if we would be able to see the baby. Ryan and I were saddened by this news we were trying to process, but we still felt so much hope. We were so full of hope that the miscarriage diagnosis was wrong and that our little baby was just hiding. We endured an exceptionally long week as we fervently prayed every day that our baby was okay. We leaned heavily on the verse of 2 Corinthians 5:7 (NLT): "For we live by believing and not by seeing."

The day we eagerly awaited finally arrived for my second ultrasound appointment. I had called the office manager at my hospital prior to my appointment to ask if my husband, Ryan, could come with me to my appointment. I explained our situation, and she told me that he could absolutely be there with me. I wept, and I thanked her for her kindness and grace. We didn't know how this day would go, but we refused to give up our hope, and we prayed without ceasing. I struggled to find the words to pray as I cried out. It's okay to not always have the words because sometimes there aren't any. Sometimes all we have are tears, and He has collected them all. Romans 8:26 (NIV) says: "The Spirit helps us in our weakness. We do not know what we ought to pray for, but the Spirit himself intercedes for us through wordless groans."

As Ryan and I walked into the doctor's office, the song that Ryan sang to me at our wedding was playing over the speakers. The song is "Promise to Love Her." I cried as I told Ryan that our song was playing. I felt so comforted that God was right there with us, and the song was God's way of letting us know that we were not alone. Exodus 14:14 (NLT) says: "The Lord himself will fight for you. Just stay calm."

I laid on the table, and as soon as the ultrasound began, there was my baby on the screen! We saw our baby and heard the loud "thump, thump" of our baby's heartbeat! Ryan and I cried as we began thanking our heavenly Father for this moment and this beautiful gift. My doctor told me that she had never experienced this, and she said she wanted to check my hormone levels and see me again in a week. She said she had a slight concern about the baby's size compared to the size of my gestational sac and the number of weeks I had been pregnant. We were not too concerned as we were filled with so much excitement that we heard our little baby's heartbeat. Friends and family began rejoicing with us with phone calls, text messages, videos, and gifts that arrived in the mail all week.

The following week showed up, and it was time for me to go back to my doctor to see how my pregnancy was progressing. Once again, Ryan had to wait in the car due to the hospital restrictions during COVID. I was so excited to see our baby's growth. As I laid on the table during the ultrasound, there was a long wait that was filled with a lot of silence. The ultrasound technician finally told me that she couldn't find our baby's heartbeat, and she left the room to get my doctor. I cried as I began talking to Ryan over a FaceTime call as I awaited my doctor to come in. Psalm 61:2 (NKJV) says: "When my heart is overwhelmed; Lead me to the rock that is higher than I."

When my doctor came in and looked at the ultrasound and examined me further, she told me that this confirms it was a miscarriage while telling me that she was so sorry. She told me that, statistically, this was quite common as one in every four pregnancies ends in a miscarriage usually due to chromosome abnormalities and that it typically happens around this time. I began crying, and then I asked her what the next steps would be. She gave me a few options of waiting for my body to recognize the miscarriage and to go through the process naturally or to schedule a surgery to remove everything so I could be finished with it and not have to endure much pain. I continued crying as I asked why this was happening, and she reassured me that it was nothing that I did, and she compassionately explained that these things just happen.

This was two days before Christmas, and I wanted to be able to put on a happy face for our family that was coming to town. I asked my doctor if I could do another ultrasound the next week to confirm before making any type of decision, and she agreed. Ryan and I also chose to do a more advanced ultrasound for our peace of mind. Ryan and I began grieving over the hopes and dreams of our little family. After more ultrasounds and second opinions, we were faced with the decision of what to do next. We made the choice to not have the surgery and to endure the miscarriage naturally. On the drive home, Ryan told me that he wanted to name our baby, "Baby Hope."

We had hope because we knew that our baby was in Heaven in the arms of our heavenly Father that loves our baby more than we ever could. We never lost our hope during the journey, and we also had hope of conceiving again. Hope is what carried us forward. 2 Kings 20:5 (NIV) says: "I have heard your prayer and seen your tears; I will heal you."

It took my body additional weeks to recognize the miscarriage, and I began having excruciating cramps. By this time, I was twelve weeks pregnant. I did not know what to expect, but Ryan and I were at home on a Sunday morning when my body went into labor. This was the most physical pain I had ever experienced as I began having contractions and vomiting. I learned that whether you're twelve weeks pregnant or forty weeks pregnant, your uterus will contract to expel what is inside. As I was experiencing this, I realized why women chose the D&C route of having medical intervention. My doctor had prescribed me pain pills to help me get through this at home. As I spent hours passing my baby, my husband never left my side. With every contraction, he would hug me as tightly as possible, and he told me he was my "toilet teddy bear." He brought me a blanket and wrapped it around me as he made sure I was comforted through the process. After hours of misery, I was finally able to get in bed with a heating pad and my husband, who took the day off work to be with me. Little did I know that I would spend the next four months enduring this traumatic experience. Matthew 11:28 (NIV) says: "Come to me, all you who are weary and burdened, and I will give you rest."

I began going to the doctor every week to check my hormone levels; it took twelve additional weeks for my hormone levels to return to normal. While going through this, I did not know that I was experiencing postpartum depression, nor did I understand what that truly was. I began going to counseling, and I also read many devotionals related to pregnancy loss. I wasn't giving myself the grace I needed, and I continued striving to please others amid my pain. I wanted to be back to normal again, and I was frustrated that I was grieving and battling the hormones that come with pregnancy. Ecclesiastes 3:1 (NKJV) says: "To everything there is a season, a time for every purpose under Heaven."

As I endured deep grief, I began spending every moment of the day with the Lord as I had so many questions. Isaiah 43:2 (NLT) says: "When you go through deep waters, I will be with you. When you go through rivers of difficulty, you will not drown. When you walk through the fire of oppression, you will not be burned up; the flames will not consume you."

Society suggests that it's best to wait until you're around three months to share your pregnancy announcement. This is because most pregnancy losses occur in the first trimester, so there is a cultural expectation that women should wait until their big news is good news. The Bible teaches us that life begins at conception, and the Lord knew us before we were ever in our mother's womb (Jeremiah 1:5 NIV).

I'm grateful that we were able to conceive as many couples endure the heartache of infertility. So, I tell my story with sensitivity toward anyone who is struggling with fertility. Although we had the hope of "trying again," we were mourning a specific soul, which was the beautiful heartbeat that we heard that mid-December day.

I couldn't be mad at God because God lives within us, and He was right there with me. He was loving on me through my husband, and He never left my side. My baby's death left me with something much greater. The divine closeness I have with my husband and the empathy and understanding I have toward women who experience pregnancy loss … that was the gift. Romans 8:18 (NLT) says: "What we suffer now is nothing compared to the glory he will reveal to us later."

I did things every day to help me through my grief such as journaling, playing the piano, taking a bubble bath, going on a bike ride, or working out as all these things teach our mind to be more present in the moment. Every morning I would wake up and write down things I was grateful for such as my husband, a safe home, my career, and the ability to work from home, but nothing compared to being in God's word. Opening my Bible was like crawling into God's lap every day. I strived to have an attitude of gratitude to magnify positive emotions and to write down how I was genuinely feeling while reframing those thoughts to build new thought patterns. I would write down all the things I was doing right as I strived to search for grace on this journey to healing. As I prayed, I heard the Lord tell me that hearing my baby's heartbeat was a divine gift to me. I believe that my baby was already gone and that God allowed me to see a glimpse of our baby and hear our baby's heartbeat from Heaven. I know that God gave me that gift to reassure us that our baby has a soul.

My counselor told me it was important to not force away any thoughts, or the thoughts will fight back. We want to "feel the thought" and then reframe the thought with what aligns with God's word. The more we do this, the more we will have new thought patterns over time. Here on earth, we will all experience trials and difficult seasons. We can all probably relate to things such as stress, anxiety, worry, or depression, but when those type of feelings consume us and control our days, that is when we know it's from the enemy and not from God. I discovered that memorizing and meditating on scripture was my cure. I say this a lot, but God's word spoken aloud is our greatest weapon.

Ryan and I decided to do a balloon release as a tribute to Baby Hope. Our families also released balloons from Arkansas and Tennessee during the same time we did. Ryan and I went to the cemetery where his dad is buried just minutes away from our home to release our balloons for Baby Hope. It was the beginning of January, and it happened to be snowing that day. It rarely snows in Texas, and someone told me that snow symbolizes healing. I was thankful for the snow as it felt as though God was embracing us with a blanket of love and support. Psalm 34:18 (NIV) says: "The Lord is close to the brokenhearted and saves those who are crushed in spirit."

A year later, we found out that we were pregnant for the second time. We were in Eureka Springs on a romantic anniversary trip when we received this news. We were elated and hopeful. This excitement and joy we were feeling after enduring such a tragedy was something that could only come from God above.

During my first doctor's appointment, we saw our baby and heard the beautiful sound of our second baby's heartbeat. I sobbed as I heard that miraculous sound. We were so excited about our "rainbow baby" and began creating a list of potential names. I was so ecstatic about the thought of being parents. I endured a lot of fatigue and sickness during this second pregnancy, and I was confident that it was reassurance that everything was progressing well.

A few weeks later at my following ultrasound appointment, my doctor confirmed that there was no longer a heartbeat. As I laid there, I said, "This feels very familiar." I felt so numb. Since I had gone through this before, I was able to make an informed decision with my next steps now that I had the knowledge I learned about pregnancy losses. After a couple of ultrasounds, I had a surgery to remove my baby at ten weeks gestation.

Once again, going through this experience brought me closer to my husband. Ryan was there by my side through it all, and as they rolled me back to take me into the surgery room, he placed his hand on the door of my room and prayed over me. We named our second little baby "RJ" after the initials of mine and Ryan's first names.

One way to rebuke the enemy from getting in our ears is to begin expressing abundant gratitude, even when it's hard to find reasons to be thankful amid heartache. After my surgery, I began praying and saying aloud:

"Thank you, Lord, for my amazing medical team."

"Thank you, God, for healing my body."

"Thank you, Father, for leading us to a specialist."

"Thank you, Jesus, for grieving with us and comforting us through it all."

We grieve over the hopes and dreams of our babies, but we continue to choose to move forward with abundant hope for the future. We can rest assured that our precious babies are in Heaven and in the arms of Jesus. Psalm 139:16 (NIV) tells us that God saw our unformed bodies. God knew us before he ever created us.

Ryan and I learned how to give ourselves grace because sadness is warranted, and it's healthy to mourn a loss. We can't wait to meet our babies one day in Heaven. Following our losses, the Lord led us to medical answers to help us sustain a future pregnancy.

Chapter 11

PEOPLE PLEASING

As soon as you begin to get on the right track, the enemy will do anything he can to distract you. The devil wants us to live for anyone other than our heavenly Father. When we start to care about someone's love, opinion, or approval more than God's, then that person becomes an idol in our lives. The Bible tells us in Exodus 20:3 (NIV): "You shall have no other gods before me." Jesus lived for an audience of one, and we must do the same.

Galatians 1:10 (NIV) says: "Am I now trying to win the approval of human beings, or of God? Or am I trying to please people? If I were trying to please people, I would not be a servant of Christ." Jesus' disciple Peter denied Jesus because he was concerned about others and the disapproval of the crowd. When God's approval matters most to us, then people will lose the grip they have over our lives. Psalm 118:8 (NLT) says: "It is better to take refuge in the Lord than to trust in people."

God shaped us to need each other. There is a spiritual gift of *encouragement*, and it's essential to development, but the desire for approval can be misused and become an obsession. It can consume our time and happiness. The desire for approval is the fear of disapproval, and it's a common reason that people get detoured and live in depression. We want to be considerate of others, but we cannot live under the stress of worrying about making everyone happy. Ephesians 5:10 (NLT) says: "Carefully determine what pleases the Lord," and Proverbs 16:7 (NLT) says: "When people's lives please the Lord, even their enemies are at peace with them."

After I experienced my first miscarriage, I began depending on family and friends around me for comfort. I was in a very vulnerable season as I was experiencing postpartum depression and anxiety without even realizing it until after the fact. It took several months for my hormone levels to return to normal, which means that it took a long time for my body to recognize that it wasn't pregnant anymore. When we expect other people to comfort us in the way we need, it will always set us up for disappointment. It's also not fair to put that kind of responsibility on someone; they will not have the ability to fully meet our needs. When we depend on someone to be there for us and tell us what we need to hear and to comfort us the way we need to be comforted, then we are asking them to do something that only God can do.

When we are in God's word and going to our heavenly Father first and foremost, then we can be more prepared when people unintentionally say hurtful things during our challenging seasons. God's word is our sword, and when we know God's truth about us, then we will have the true comfort we need during our darkest days. The more important Jesus is to you, the more it will set you free, and you will be delivered from the fear of disapproval. God uses truth, and the truth will set you free. John 8:36 (NLT) says: "So if the Son sets you free, you will be free indeed."

One of the primary areas of my life where I found myself focused on pleasing people was my place of employment. We spend most of our time at work among our colleagues. As I worked hard to move up into management and create my own team of employees, I found myself more focused on work than ever before. Proverbs 29:25 (NLT) says: "Fearing people is a dangerous trap, but trusting the Lord means safety." The Lord wants us to work hard and to be a light wherever we go as Ephesians 6:7 (NLT) says: "Work with enthusiasm, as though you were working for the Lord rather than for people," and Colossians 3:23 (NLT) says: "Work willingly at whatever you do, as though you were working for the Lord rather than for people." Our purpose is to please God, not people as 1 Thessalonians 2:4 (NLT) says: "He examines the motives of our hearts."

People pleasing is also an indicator of insecurity. God's approval sets us free from insecurity because our Lord will never reject us. God promises to never forsake us and to never reject us. Psalm 27:10 (NLT) says: "Even if my father and mother abandon me, the Lord will hold me close."

The most common people we probably try to please are our parents or parental figures in our lives. While we want to honor our father and mother as we are instructed to do so in many verses throughout the Bible, including Deuteronomy 5:16 (NTL), we must not allow this striving of honoring them to cause us to enter a place where we revolve our lives around making them proud before doing what pleases the Lord. Matthew 10:37 (NIV) says: "Anyone who loves their father or mother more than me is not worthy of me; anyone who loves their son or daughter more than me is not worthy of me." God must remain on the pedestal above all else including the people and things we love the most in this world. 1 Corinthians 7:31 (NLT) says: "Those who use the things of the world should not become attached to them. For this world as we know it will soon pass away."

If we remain concerned about pleasing people, then it will emotionally disable us, and we will allow disapproval to manipulate us. We must break free from the trap of people pleasing. One way we can break free is to change the way we think. We must repent. Repentance simply means to "change our minds." Romans 12:2 (NIV) says: "Do not conform to the pattern of this world but be transformed by the renewing of your mind. Then you will be able to test and approve what God's will is—His good, pleasing, and perfect will."

People pleasing can cause us to miss out on God's plan for our lives. Luke 6:26 (NLT) says: "What sorrow awaits you who are praised by the crowds." We long to feel accepted and approved by others, but Proverbs 25:27 (NLT) says: "It's not good to eat too much honey, and it's not good to seek honors for yourself." If we start to live for validation, recognition, and approval, then we will lose focus of what it means to do good. In 1 Samuel 15:24 (NLT) Saul admitted to Samuel and said, "Yes, I have sinned. I have disobeyed your instructions and the Lord's command, for I was afraid of the people and did what they demanded."

2 Timothy 2:15 (NLT) says: "Work hard so you can present yourself to God and receive His approval. Be a good worker, one who does not need to be ashamed and who correctly explains the word of truth." Satan also loves to silence people. John 7:13 (NLT) says: "No one had the courage to speak favorably about Him in public out of fear of the leaders." Luke 9:26 (NLT) says: "If anyone is ashamed of me and my message, the Son of Man will be ashamed of that person when He returns."

We don't want to please people by following the crowd by doing wrong. If bad companions tempt us, then we do not need to surround ourselves with them. Do not be misled as 1 Corinthians 15:33 (NIV) says: "Bad company corrupts good character."

To follow the Lord wholeheartedly, you will need to release your desire to please others. You can still be a blessing to other people as God enables you to reflect His light in this dark world.

Dear Father God,

Please deliver us from the sin of people pleasing. Help us to stay focused on Your will for our lives. Please guide us into what pleases You more than anything else. If we drift away with the desire of seeking praise or affirmation, please pull us back to You, God. We want to make You proud. We love you, Father, and we ask for Your deliverance from people pleasing.

In Your Son's Name,
Amen

Chapter 12

URGENCY

God wants us to have childlike faith. Luke 18:17 (NIV) says: "Truly I tell you, anyone, who will not receive the Kingdom of God like a little child will never enter it." When we release our cares to our heavenly Father, it shows Him that we trust Him, and He wants to handle our battles for us. Just like a toddler depends on his or her parent, God wants us to depend on Him in that same way. We can learn so much from little children when it comes to their faith.

After Richard passed away, I would get so many little signs from God, whether it was a yellow butterfly, a Bible verse I needed to hear that day, or a song on the radio. When I started to open myself up to the possibility of what I couldn't understand and when I was willing to have a childlike faith, God's love kept flowing through. Some little gifts were obvious, and some were subtle, but with each gift,

I found peace to keep moving forward with this beautiful thing called "life."

We can study God's word and read the Bible each day, but it's a wonderful thing when we allow ourselves to truly experience God's love and comfort through His Holy Spirit.

One Wednesday evening during the weekly prayer call with our church, our prayer pastor began specifically praying for us to all have a sense of urgency. An urgency to run to the Lord. An urgency to run to our Abba before we run to our spouse, our sister, our brother, our friend, or our parent. An urgency to run to our heavenly Father first.

The word *urgency* became life-changing for me. What an overwhelming sense of peace we receive when we run to our Father God with that urgency. The Lord wants us to run to Him with our good news, bad news, concerns, prayers, petitions, and praises.

A story in the Bible, in Luke 17:12–19 (NIV), says that "As Jesus was going into a village, ten men who had leprosy met him. They stood at a distance and called out in a loud voice, "Jesus, Master, have pity on us!" When Jesus saw them, he said, "Go, show yourselves to the priests." And as they went, they were cleansed. One of them, when he saw he was healed, came back, praising God in a loud voice. He threw himself at Jesus' feet and thanked him. Jesus asked, "Were not all ten cleansed? Where are the other nine? Has no one returned to give praise to God except this foreigner?" Then he said to him, "Rise and go; your faith has made you well."

That story blows my mind that only one man came back to thank Jesus. It has me reflecting on all the gifts I've received and didn't go back to thank Jesus, or perhaps I updated everyone else by thanking them for their prayers, but I didn't go back to our Father to personally thank Him specifically first and foremost.

When we consistently run to our heavenly Father with a sense of urgency, then that will help us maintain our number one priority of keeping God above all else.

Chapter 13

SUFFERING WELL

We will all have pain in this life because it's not optional. Misery is optional, but experiencing pain is not optional. On earth, the struggle will never be gone completely, so if I must suffer, I just want to suffer well. We can run to God or run away from God. I have spent more time with God through my darkest days. That time alone with God has kept me going.

Did you know that crying out to God is an act of worship? God doesn't want us to say what we think we should say to Him. Paul, in the Bible, gives us a notable example of authenticity. Paul said they were crushed and overwhelmed and saw how powerless they were, so they put everything into the hands of God who could help them.

Our prayers get a lot more real when we are hurting. Many of us can say that pain turned us to Christ. Paul says in 2 Corinthians 7:9 (NLT): "I'm glad, not because the pain hurt you but because the pain turned you to God." Proverbs 20:30 (GNT) says: "Sometimes it takes a painful experience to change our ways."

No one is promised an easy life, not even Christians. We are all created to become like Jesus Christ. Hebrews 5:8 (NLT) says: "Even though Jesus was God's Son, He learned obedience from the things he suffered." Suffering is what made Jesus perfect, as there are some things we only learn through our pain. God has given us the gift of fragility, which is an opportunity for us to blossom in His presence. Rather than denying our weakness, we can allow God to bless us richly through it.

The first step in healing is to stay close to God. The closer we stay to Him, the more He will reveal to us, and the remarkable thing is Romans 8:34 (NIV) says: "Jesus is at the right hand of God, and He is interceding and pleading for us." Psalm 147:3 (NIV) says: "God heals the brokenhearted and binds up their wounds."

Whatever type of pain you're going through—whether it's spiritual, emotional, financial, relational, physical—we are far better prepared to manage it if we focus on the purpose of the pain. God can bring much good out of the most painful situations. God will use our pain to fulfill His purpose. Most people waste their suffering, and therefore Paul asks the question in Galatians 3:4 (NLT): "Have you experienced so much for nothing?" Human beings can handle an unbelievable amount of pain if they're able to see the purpose in it. Purposeless pain wears us down.

Pain always transforms us. But we either get better or we get bitter. If we can be mature enough, then the pain will deepen our love. Suffering sensitizes us. I have seen pain turn very selfish people into very sympathetic people. All you must do is go through some pain yourself, and you develop the gift of having empathy toward others. If we use God's purpose with our pain, then it'll make us better and not bitter.

Pain is an opportunity to grow in our character. How does God produce the fruit of the spirit? God produces His fruit in us when we are in the exact opposite situation. How is God going to teach us joy? Through our sorrow. If you've been abused your whole life, then God's going to put some loving and sensitive people on your path to teach you love. If you've had a great life, then He may put some difficult people on your path to teach you patience. We do not develop the fruit of the spirit by just believing. We develop the fruit through our character development throughout our journey. We become resilient people when we have pain in our lives. Romans 5:3–4 (ESV) says: "We rejoice in our sufferings, knowing that suffering produces endurance, and endurance produces character, and character produces hope."

Our Spirit is renewed day by day. These temporary troubles will bring us eternal glory, which is much better than the troubles. We need to fix our attention on what is unseen because what is unseen lasts forever and gives us an eternal perspective. Christ endured the cross because He was able to look past the pain to the purpose.

Sometimes Christians think the world is impressed by

how we enjoy prosperity. Some think if people see believers living large, then everyone will want to become a Christian. The truth is that people are not impressed with prosperity. Unbelievers are impressed with how Christians handle adversity. Our suffering gives us character and credibility. Paul was a pro at using his pain to be a witness. Philippians 1:2 (NLT) says: "I want you to know, my dear brothers and sisters, that everything that has happened to me here has helped to spread the Good News."

2 Corinthians 6:4 (NLT) says: "In everything we do, we show that we are true ministers of God. We patiently endure troubles and hardships and calamities of every kind." Our deepest life message will come out of our deepest pain. Every area in our life where we've had pain is a testimony to share with others. There are people out there going through the pain we've gone through, and they need us, so we cannot waste our hurt.

Someone once asked me, "How can you not be angry at God for your pregnancy losses?" I responded with, "How can I be angry at God? He was right there with me, loving on me through it all." He never left my side, and I'm so thankful. 2 Corinthians 1:4 (NLT) says: "God comforts us in all our troubles so that we can comfort others. When they are troubled, we will be able to give them the same comfort God has given us."

Jesus wants to redeem our suffering so that we are healed and equipped to help others. Who can better help someone that is going through something difficult than someone that's gone through that similar pain? The thing that hurt us the most in our life will become our greatest ministry. God doesn't want us to waste our pain. We think we help people in our strengths, but we help people through our weaknesses because that's when people can relate to us. If we lived a perfect life, then how would we be able to help anyone? Jesus is also right there with us when we are helping others as He tells us in Matthew 18:20 (ESV): "For where two or three are gathered in my name, there am I among them."

I had a friend say to me once, "It's been an honor to struggle with you." If we must strive to struggle well, then let's struggle together and help carry each other's load so that nobody falls behind. 2 Timothy 2:3 (ESV) says: "Share in suffering as a good soldier of Christ Jesus." We are called to be there for others in fellowship through the hills and the valleys as Romans 12:15 (NIV) tells us: "Rejoice with those who rejoice; mourn with those who mourn." We are all spiritual beings that are having a human experience. 2 Corinthians 4:10 (NLT) says: "Through suffering, our bodies continue to share in the death of Jesus so that the life of Jesus may also be seen in our bodies."

You may be wondering how you can be there for someone who is struggling and suffering. The deeper someone is in pain, the fewer words we should use. What people need is the ministry of presence. We don't get over grief; we must go through it, and there's no right or wrong way.

We also should never try to invalidate how other people feel or what they think because that will never produce a good result. If we try to invalidate what someone is going through, then that will put them in defense mode. When we validate how someone feels, it releases a feel-good chemical in their brain that relaxes them, and they will be more likely to open up to us.

Sadness is warranted, and feelings are always valid. Feelings aren't right or wrong; they're just feelings, and it's important to process them. We must sit in our bad days. We have the right to be sad. If we can't be sad when a loved one dies or when we go through some sort of tragedy, then when can we be sad? We must give ourselves permission to lean into our grief. That is the healthy way to grieve. When others don't understand how we feel, that doesn't mean our feelings are wrong. James 4:6 (NLT) says: "God opposes the proud but gives grace to the humble."

I have also learned to never try to cheer someone up in the middle of their grief or suffering. The best thing we can do is walk over to them and put our arms around them and be there for them. That's grace. So many times, we try to find the perfect words to say, but the fellowship of suffering together is simply being together. Galatians 6:2 (NIV) says: "Carry each other's burdens, and in this way, you will fulfill the law of Christ." What is the law of Christ? James 2:8 (NIV): "Love your neighbor as yourself."

1 Peter is such a great book in the Bible about suffering. Peter is such an encourager and his letter to us is a manual on how a Christian should live in the face of discouragement and suffering. When bad things happen, 1 Peter is a great book to open up!

Peter knew what it was like to be afraid for his life as a disciple of Jesus. He denied knowing Jesus three times. Then he learned how to stand firm in an evil world, so he wanted to encourage us to do the same!

No one wants to be hurt, but when we are, it is encouraging to remember that Jesus is there to comfort us in the midst of our difficulties. Even through tough times, Christians should imitate Jesus in all of our relationships. Peter's letter helps us understand why we suffer and tells us how suffering refines our faith. Ultimately, it shows the hope all believers have. The good news is: our suffering will one day end when we are ushered into God's heavenly Kingdom!

Peter tells us to be truly glad because there is wonderful joy ahead. He says that even though we must endure many trials for a little while, these trials will show that our faith is genuine. He said that our faith is being tested as fire tests and purifies gold, but our faith is more precious than gold. Our reward for trusting God will be the salvation of our souls!

As you endure any kind of suffering in this life, please remember to take care of yourselves through the process by being in God's word, moving your body, journaling, seeking support, eating well, resting, and doing things that feel good, comforting, and soothing. Remember to breathe and take it one day, one hour, one minute at a time if you need to. You can do this. You can do hard things.

> Sorrow is better than laughter, for by a sad
> countenance the heart is made better.
>
> —Ecclesiastes 7:3 (NKJV)

Chapter 14

THE POWER OF WORDS

Proverbs 18:21 (NLT) says: "The tongue has the power of life and death."

Our tongue is the most powerful part of our bodies. We can use our tongues to tear people down or to build each other up. We can use our tongues to speak blessings or to speak curses. Matthew 12:34 (NIV) says: "The mouth speaks what the heart is full of."

How would we speak if we knew that our words could impact the future of the people we love? What would we start saying? Our words are like seeds that are planted into the hearts of others. We can ask ourselves, "Am I using my words to bless others or to remind them of their weaknesses and shortcomings?" The words we decide to use can also be a bridge to someone's heart.

Among all creatures in creation, the Lord gave human

beings the beautiful gift of using our tongues to communicate with verbal language. We all have the power of free will to choose the things we say. Proverbs 18:20–21 (NLT) says: "Wise words satisfy like a good meal; the right words bring satisfaction," and Proverbs 12:18 (NIV) says: "The words of the reckless pierce like swords, but the tongue of the wise brings healing." We have the power to choose how we will use the gift of our words.

James 3:7–11 (NLT) says: "People can tame all kinds of animals, birds, reptiles, and fish, but no one can tame the tongue. It is restless and evil, full of deadly poison. Sometimes it praises our Lord, and sometimes it curses those who have been made in the image of God. And so, blessing and cursing come pouring out of the same mouth. Surely, my brothers and sisters, this is not right!"

The tongue is the most challenging part of our bodies to control. We cannot praise God in one breath and gossip with the next breath. "No man can tame his tongue," therefore, we must repent, pray, and allow God to do the work in us. James 3:6 (NLT) says: "Among all the parts of the body, the tongue is a flame of fire. It is a whole world of wickedness, corrupting your entire body."

Isaiah 6:5–7 (NLT) says: "I am doomed, for I am a sinful man. I have filthy lips, and I live among people with filthy lips. Yet I have seen the King, the Lord of Heaven's Armies. Then one of the seraphim flew to me with a burning coal he had taken from the altar with a pair of tongs. He touched my lips with it and said, "See, this coal has touched your lips. Now your guilt is removed, and your sins are forgiven."

God has equipped us with what we need, and He asks us to speak His word. Ephesians 6:17 (NIV) says: "Take the helmet of salvation and the sword of the Spirit, which is the word of God." We must speak the word of God aloud especially during our tough times. We must not say how we feel or what people tell us but what God has told us. I have learned that complaining is a sin, and when we do it, we open the door for the enemy to enter our lives. Ephesians 6:11 (NIV) says: "Put on the full armor of God so that you can take your stand against the devil's schemes."

We must be careful that we don't allow the devil to talk us out of what God has planned for our lives. We can kill the power of God by speaking things that are not in agreement with God's plan. We must fight the enemy when he tries to detour us. Luke 10:19 (NIV) says: "I have given you authority to trample on snakes and scorpions and to overcome all the power of the enemy; nothing will harm you."

Hebrews 4:12 (NLT) says: "For the word of God is alive and powerful. It is sharper than the sharpest two-edged sword, cutting between soul and spirit, between joint and marrow. It exposes our innermost thoughts and desires."

We can easily see where people are on their walk with God by listening to the way they talk. Are they saying hateful words or loving words? Are they gossiping or encouraging? Are they complaining or praising? Ephesians 4:29 (NIV) says: "Do not let any unwholesome talk come out of your mouths, but only what is helpful for building others up according to their needs, that it may benefit those who listen."

There's a cool story in the Bible in Luke 1:11–22 (NLT):

> While Zechariah was in the sanctuary, an angel of the Lord appeared to him, standing to the right of the incense altar. Zechariah was shaken and overwhelmed with fear when he saw him. But the angel said, "Don't be afraid, Zechariah! God has heard your prayer. Your wife, Elizabeth, will give you a son, and you are to name him John. You will have great joy and gladness, and many will rejoice at his birth, for he will be great in the eyes of the Lord. He must never touch wine or other alcoholic drinks. He will be filled with the Holy Spirit, even before his birth. And he will turn many Israelites to the Lord their God. He will be a man with the spirit and power of Elijah. He will prepare the people for the coming of the Lord. He will turn the hearts of the fathers to their children, and he will cause those who are rebellious to accept the wisdom of the godly." Zechariah said to the angel, "How can I be sure this will happen? I'm an old man now, and my wife is also well along in years." Then the angel said, "I am Gabriel! I stand in the very presence of God. It was he who sent me to bring you this Good News! But now, since you didn't believe what I said, you will be silent and unable to speak until the child is born. For my words will certainly be fulfilled

at the proper time." Meanwhile, the people were waiting for Zechariah to come out of the sanctuary, wondering why he was taking so long. When he finally did come out, he couldn't speak to them. Then they realized from his gestures and his silence that he must have seen a vision in the sanctuary.

God had to supernaturally shut Zachariah's mouth because this man was not verbally cooperating with God's plan. How many of us have messed up what God has planned by saying things we shouldn't say? I love the story of Zechariah because much can be learned through that message. The angel was telling Zechariah that his wife would be pregnant with a forerunner for Jesus, but Zechariah still had doubts. The Bible tells us that many miracles were not performed because of disbelief. I've been on this mission of speaking life over my circumstances and fully believing without doubting.

When we lost our second baby in the womb, I had people tell me that the enemy was out to get me. Of course, the enemy was out to get me because if we are serving God, then we are a huge threat to him. Rather than allowing the enemy to collect a trophy for the depression I was feeling after losing my babies, I began thanking the Lord aloud with my words. "Thank you, Lord, for allowing us to hear their heartbeats. Thank You, God, for healing my body. Thank you, Father, for my medical team."

1 Thessalonians 5:16–18 (NIV) tells us: "Rejoice always, pray continually, and give thanks in all circumstances." Those keywords "always," "continually," and "all"—mean to praise

God no matter what comes your way. Philippians 4:4 (NIV) says: "Rejoice in the Lord always." There is always something to be thankful for, and may we always acknowledge all the little blessings and miracles amid trials and heartache. I heard Joyce Meyer say, "Complain and remain or praise and be raised!"

We also have the power to speak life or death over other people. When we treat someone the way he is, then he will remain how he is, but when we treat someone as they could and should be, then they become as they could and should be. Hebrews 10:24–25 (NLT) says: "Let us think of ways to motivate one another to acts of love and good works." And 1 Thessalonians 5:11 (NIV) tells us to "encourage one another and build each other up!"

We can also bless others in our simple conversations or group discussions. If conversations get heated, the Bible gives us instructions on how to manage those situations. Proverbs 15:1 (NLT) says: "A gentle answer deflects anger, but harsh words make tempers flare." And James 1:19 (NIV) says: "My dear brothers and sisters, take note of this: Everyone should be quick to listen, slow to speak, and slow to become angry."

Most of the time, the best thing we can do is to stay silent and hold back our words to prevent causing pain or regret. We don't always have to have an answer or strive to search for the perfect words. Proverbs 17:38 (NLT) says: "Even fools are thought wise when they keep silent; with their mouths shut, they seem intelligent." We must be careful, wise, and selective when we do choose to speak because Matthew 12:36 (NIV) says: "I tell you that everyone will have to give account on the day of judgment for every empty word they have spoken."

We also need to use our words to speak up for others in a godly way. Proverbs 31:8 (NLT) says: "Speak up for those who cannot speak for themselves; ensure justice for those being crushed." Our action of standing up for others will show that we love them as 1 John 3:18 (NLT) says: "Dear children, let's not merely say that we love each other; let us show the truth by our actions."

The best thing we can do with our tongue and our mouth is to praise our heavenly Father and to speak His truth to others. Psalm 100:2 (NLT) says: "Worship the Lord with gladness. Come before him, singing with joy," and John 15:7 (NLT) says: "But if you remain in me and my words remain in you, you may ask for anything you want, and it will be granted!" We must use our tongues to communicate with our heavenly Father. He loves the sound of your voice because He created it. He wants us to use our words to talk with Him. James 4:2 (NIV) says: "You do not have because you do not ask God."

Peter tells us in 1 Peter that if we want to enjoy life and see many happy days, then we must keep our tongue from speaking evil and we must do good. He tells us to search for peace and work to maintain it.

Peter also tells us to exercise self-control and to not slip back into old ways of living. He tells us we should all be of one mind, sympathizing with each other and loving each other as brothers and sisters. He tells us to be tenderhearted, and to keep a humble attitude and not to repay evil for evil or retaliate with insults when people insult us. He tells us to pay them back with a *blessing*.

Chapter 15

CHOOSING JOY

The word *joy* is found in the Bible over 150 times, and I have made it my mission to learn the difference between happiness and joy. Happiness is situational, based on "happenings," but joy is a fruit of the Spirit regardless of circumstances. Real joy comes through a relationship with Jesus! Real joy never dims, no matter what life throws at us because we are loved and chosen by God, and we will live with Him forever in Heaven.

Philippians is one of my favorite books in the Bible because Paul was our model for joy. Paul was in prison and in chains for sharing the gospel and he was all alone except for an occasional visitor. The book of Philippians is Paul's letter of joy and to always be full of joy in the Lord no matter what is happening. Paul told us in his letter, "whatever happens, always rejoice in the Lord."

Although Paul was enduring adversity, he said that everything that happened to him helped him spread the Good News. Paul told us that God who began the good work within us will continue His work until it is finished. Paul was the epitome of joy regardless of circumstances.

A lot of people think that the "abundant life" that God refers to means materialistic possessions, big houses, fancy cars, expensive jewelry, or high-paying careers, but did you know that having joy means that you are experiencing the abundant life to which God is referring? Galatians 5:22 (NLT) says: "The Holy Spirit produces this kind of fruit in our lives: love, joy, peace, patience, kindness, goodness, faithfulness, gentleness, and self-control." When we choose Jesus, we are choosing for the Holy Spirit to live within us and give us joy. Joy is the deepest part of a person who has accepted Jesus. Paul said that he learned to be content with what he had which is such a great reminder to us. He said that he learned how to live on almost nothing or with everything because he had the Lord. He reminded us that God will always supply all of our needs.

Psalm 16:11 (NLT) says: "You will show me the way of life, granting me the joy of your presence and the pleasures of living with you forever."

If the Lord never gives me another blessing in my life, I will praise Him each morning for the mere fact that I opened my eyes! Psalm 118:24 (BSB) says: "This is the day that the Lord has made; we will rejoice and be glad in it." I get to wake up each morning with my husband by my side, and every day I am thankful and filled with joy. The man I prayed for is now the man I pray with! We can easily get caught up with life and our desires and overlook the blessings all around us. We must remember not to get too focused on the future that we forget to stop and realize that today is what we prayed for years ago.

Those who feel joy from our Lord are filled with hope, faith, and love regardless of their circumstances. Joy is a fruit of the Spirit and a choice to us. People can't rob your joy unless you allow it. People cannot control our emotions unless we let them. Deuteronomy 30:19 (NIV) says: "I call Heaven and earth to witness this day against you that I have set before you life and death. Blessings and curses, so *choose* life so that you and your descendants may live."

You may be wondering how to find joy when you're around some joy deflators. Ephesians 4:2–3 (NLT) says: "Always be humble and gentle. Be patient with each other, making allowance for each other's faults because of your love," and John 13:34–35 (NLT) says: "So now I am giving you a new commandment: Love each other. Just as I have loved you, you should love each other. Your love for one another will prove to the world that you are my disciples."

People who need the most love will ask for it in the most unloving ways. If people are rude, unkind, impatient, or angry toward us, we must love them through it. The Bible tells us in Romans 12:14 (NLT): "Bless those who persecute you. Don't curse them; pray that God will bless them." We never know what someone is battling, and we are called to show them Christ's love and to be gentle.

If someone hurts us, we must forgive him or her to

maintain our joy. Matthew 18:21–22 (NIV) says: "Then Peter came and said to Him, "Lord, how often shall my brother sin against me and I forgive him? Up to seven times?" Jesus said to him, "I do not say to you, up to seven times, but up to seventy times seven."

It's okay to get angry but do not justify sin because of anger as the Bible says in Ephesians 4:26-27 (ESV): "Be angry and do not sin; do not let the sun go down on your anger and give no opportunity to the devil." Anger is a normal, healthy emotion. We have God-given emotions that teach us things, and anger is our mind's beautiful way of trying to protect itself. There's nothing wrong with today's anger. Yesterday's anger is the problem. Yesterday's anger causes destruction. The healthiest thing we can do is to never go to bed angry. Today's anger is manageable. The devil does not have access to today's anger. When you go to bed on anger, the devil slithers in, and you give him an open door to deceive you.

John 10:10 (NIV) says: "The thief comes only to steal and kill and destroy; I have come that they may have life and have it to the full." To stay strong, we must also stay joyful. Joy is a great weapon against the enemy, as he sure does hate when we are filled with joy. What an excellent way to rebuke him. Colossians 1:11 (ASV) says: "We are strengthened with all power, according to the might of His glory, unto all patience and long-suffering with *joy*."

We are children of God; sons and daughters of the King, and the devil wants to kill our inner child. Our inner child gives us our childlike faith, and the enemy wants to destroy that and fill us with worry and fear. 1 John 4:4 (NLT) says:

"You belong to God, my dear children. You have already won a victory over those people because the Spirit who lives in you is greater than the spirit who lives in the world."

We can dream about what we think our life should look like, but we all know that comparison is the thief of joy. Comparison is a tool of the enemy. The Bible tells us that we will have trouble in this world. It won't be long before we are faced with another problem, so we can't hold back to start enjoying our life. We must choose joy amid our troubles. Joy is a low-hanging fruit that is available to us every day. Proverbs 17:22 (ESV) says: "A joyful heart is good medicine, but a crushed spirit dries up the bones."

One day we will look back with a clearer perspective, and if our joy during our struggles brought someone else closer to Jesus, then that's the true joy.

Chapter 16

THE WAITING

The "waiting season" can be so grueling and seem like it's never-ending. Whatever it is that you're waiting for—whether it's a relationship, acceptance into a college, a dream career, a promotion, a wedding, a home, a baby, a career, a trip, or anything it may be—there will always be a period of waiting. That's where the phrase "it's worth the wait" comes from as we all know what it feels like to have to wait for a new door to open.

Matthew 6:33 (NLT) says: "Seek the Kingdom of God above all else and live righteously, and He will give you everything you need." This is such a great reminder to fix our eyes on God and to live our lives according to His word and His commandments for us. Sometimes the waiting season is a great reminder to redirect our focus to ensure that our priorities align with God's will for us. Remember that anything we love or make a priority over God can easily become an idol in our lives. The devil loves to get us fixated on anything other than our Creator. We can still have hopes, dreams, and set goals, as the Lord will put those beautiful desires in our hearts, but this is your reminder to seek God and His kingdom first, and then everything else will be given to you if it aligns with His will for your life.

The enemy has a way of slithering in during our waiting season to try to make us doubt the thing we are waiting for. The devil wants us to think that if our prayer isn't promptly answered or answered the right way, then God is not listening, or He doesn't care, or it's just not meant to be. Satan will do everything he can to make us give up and move on from the thing we are praying for and waiting for.

One of my favorite parables in the Bible is the parable about the persistent widow who kept going before the judge and asking him for justice. You can find this parable in Luke 18:1–8 (NLT):

> There was a judge in a certain city, who neither feared God nor cared about people. A widow of that city came to him repeatedly, saying, "Give me justice in this dispute with my enemy." The judge ignored her for a while, but finally he said to himself, "I don't fear God or care about people, but this woman is driving me crazy. I'm going to see that she gets justice, because she is wearing me out with her constant requests!" Then the Lord

said, "Learn a lesson from this unjust judge. Even he rendered a just decision in the end. So, don't you think God will surely give justice to his chosen people who cry out to him day and night? Will he keep putting them off? I tell you; He will grant justice to them quickly!"

Jesus told this parable so that we will always pray and never give up! God asks for us to be tenacious. Whatever you might be enduring or desiring, I hope that story inspires you to continue praying and asking no matter what. God doesn't seem to have a watch, but he does hear our prayers, and He reassures us in Isaiah 60:22 (NLT) that at the right time, He will make it happen!

My husband, Ryan, waited thirty-nine years to find me. He was forty years old when he stood at the altar and watched his bride walk down the aisle. If you are a young person looking for love, then I hope that doesn't discourage you that it may take that long, but I pray that it encourages you to keep praying and asking the Lord. Ryan never stopped praying for me; he never gave up. After Ryan and I got married, and I began meeting his extended family, they would say to me, "How does it feel to be an answered prayer?" Ryan's entire family never stopped praying for his future wife when they could have easily given up on that prayer over the years.

During my season of waiting for what was next, I left a high-paying company and later took a new career position, bought a new home, and sold my previous home. While I was doing that, Ryan was being obedient to the Lord by selling his airplane to pay off his house and to make room for what God had in store. (All while we hadn't even met yet!) Ryan tells me that the Lord told him to sell his airplane because he would never find a wife if he was always in the hangar tinkering with his plane. Ryan and I were in our waiting seasons at the same time, praying for one another, listening to the Lord, being obedient, and preparing for one another without even knowing it. It was a challenging season of change, but I knew the Lord had something amazing planned for me, so I remained steadfast.

If you are praying and waiting for other blessings in your life, here is a prayer to pray today: "Dear Lord, before I ask you for any more blessings, please help me to see all the ones right in front of me. Thank you, God, for all the goodness in my life. You are a good Father, and Your timing is perfect. In Jesus' Mighty Name, Amen."

After suffering from two pregnancy losses two holiday seasons in a row, a friend encouraged Ryan and I to do something fun that I wouldn't have been able to do if I were pregnant, such as skiing. We took that advice to heart and booked a Christmas trip to Disney World and Universal Studios in Orlando, Florida. I share that to inspire you to find meaningful things to do during your waiting season. That is one of the reasons I wrote this book. Many months after my second pregnancy loss, I heard the Lord tell me that this is my waiting season, and He told me to use that season to write this book.

The waiting season is when I become more aware and thankful for how far I've come in life, especially in my prayer life. When we are in pain, we don't have the energy for surface-level prayers. It is in our suffering and our waiting that we truly know Jesus. Perhaps your waiting season can be more of an intimate time with the Lord.

1 Peter 5:6 (NIV) tells us to "humble ourselves under God's mighty hand and He will lift us up in due time." The waiting season is the perfect time to ask the Lord to open your eyes to see all the little blessings around you. We all have our own definitions of "rich," and I learned that my definition of "rich" is my beautiful marriage. I'm so rich in love, contentment, peace, protection, security, hope, and laughter. Those are gifts of the abundant life that the Lord refers to, and I never want to take a day or any of His gifts for granted. What are some ways that the Lord has richly blessed you?

The waiting season also strengthens our faith. Hebrews 11:1 (NLT) says: "Faith shows the reality of what we hope for; it is the evidence of things we cannot see." And Romans 15:13 (NIV) says: "May the God of hope fill you with all joy and peace as you trust in Him, so that you may overflow with hope by the power of the Holy Spirit."

Whatever you may be waiting for, I pray that you can embrace what the Lord has done in your life up to this point. The blessings we receive from God are an extension of God's love, not the essence of His love. Take this time to enjoy what is around you. You are complete right now at this moment through Christ Jesus. When we hear Satan's lies that we need the thing we are waiting on to be complete, then we need to shut that door on the enemy. We can still pray and ask for those desires of our hearts if we are mindful that those desires do not consume us or define our identity.

The waiting season is a wonderful time to be more sensitive to hearing the Lord's voice. We learn in 1 Corinthians 14:33 (NIV) that God is not a God of disorder, chaos, or confusion. God is a problem-solver. God is working on your behalf, and He is telling you about some things in this waiting season to show you the clear path ahead. The enemy has a plan for our lives, and God has a plan for our lives. We must remain steadfast in prayer to know the difference.

So far you haven't asked for anything
in my name. Keep asking and you will
receive, so that your joy may be complete.

—John 16:24 (ISV)

Chapter 17

IS SATAN OUT TO GET ME?

A lot of people may wonder how Satan works and who he is after in this world. It may be natural to think that the devil is hanging out with the ones that are not followers of Jesus and people that are doing wrong things. That is not the case because Satan already has those people where he wants them. So, if we feel like Satan is out to get us then that means we are doing something good in the world. Christians are Satan's prime targets because he is deeply threatened by their Kingdom work.

Even Jesus was tempted by the enemy. In Matthew 4:1–11 (NLT), the Spirit led Jesus into the wilderness to be tempted there by the devil. For forty days and forty nights, he fasted and became very hungry. During that time, the devil came and said to him, "If you are the Son of God, tell these stones to become loaves of bread." But Jesus told him, "No! The

Scriptures say: People do not live by bread alone, but by every word that comes from the mouth of God." Then the devil took him to the holy city, Jerusalem, to the highest point of the temple, and said, "If you are the Son of God, jump off! For the Scriptures say: He will order his angels to protect you and they will hold you up with their hands, so you won't even hurt your foot on a stone." Jesus responded, "The Scriptures also say: You must not test the LORD your God." Next, the devil took him to the peak of an extremely high mountain and showed him all the kingdoms of the world and their glory. "I will give it all to you," he said, "if you will kneel down and worship me." "Get out of here, Satan," Jesus told him. "For the Scriptures say: You must worship the Lord your God and serve only Him." Then the devil went away, and angels came and took care of Jesus.

God's word spoken aloud is our greatest weapon as the Bible tells us that God's word is our sword to fight against the evil one. The enemy comes to kill, steal, and destroy. If you have happiness, he wants to kill it. If you have joy, he wants to steal it. If you have a family, he wants to destroy it. 1 Peter 5:9 (NIV) says: "Resist him, standing firm in the faith, because you know that the family of believers throughout the world is undergoing the same kind of sufferings."

If Satan is out to get you, then that is a compliment to you because he knows you're worth something, and he knows that the Lord plans to use you in a mighty way. But guess what? The God who formed you says: "Do not be afraid, for I have ransomed you. I have called you by name; you are Mine" (Isaiah 43:1 NLT).

God has given us everything we need to defeat the enemy. Ephesians 6:13–17 (NLT) tells us: "Therefore, put on every piece of God's armor so you will be able to resist the enemy in the time of evil. Then after the battle, you will still be standing firm. Stand your ground, putting on the belt of truth and the body armor of God's righteousness. For shoes, put on the peace that comes from the Good News so that you will be fully prepared. In addition to all these, hold up the shield of faith to stop the fiery arrows of the devil. Put on salvation as your helmet, and take the *sword* of the Spirit, which is the *Word of God*."

Chapter 18

PROTECT YOUR PEACE

*P*eace is a precious gift to us. 1 Peter 3:11 (NIV) tells us to "seek peace and pursue it." Jesus is the Prince of Peace. We don't have to pray for peace because Jesus is peace, and His gift is available for us to receive it. We must pray that we will walk in the peace He's already given us. Rather than praying for joy, we need to say, "I believe your joy is in me. Teach me how to not let the devil steal my joy."

Our peace is in our control. We have the power to dismiss what may be interrupting our peace as we keep God at the top of our priority list. We can protect our peace by choosing the right people to surround ourselves with. Proverbs 13:20 (NIV) says: "Walk with the wise and become wise, for a companion of fools suffers harm." Proverbs 27:17 (NLT) says: "As iron sharpens iron, so a friend sharpens a friend." Godly friends that draw you closer to God are a marvelous gift. It is so important to find friends that are trustworthy and full of wisdom and encouragement.

One of the major ways my husband and I have protected our peace is by committing to attending our church every week. Hebrews 10:24–25 (NLT) tells us: "Let us think of ways to motivate one another to acts of love and good works and let us not neglect our meeting together, as some people do, but encourage one another, especially now that the day of His return is drawing near." Attending church consistently shows that God is your number one priority, and when you spend quality time with other believers, it will help you grow your relationship with the Lord, and He is our Prince of Peace. Job 22:21 (NLT) says: "Submit to God, and you will have peace."

If we want good friends and the right friends, then we are better off not picking them out ourselves but asking God for divine connections. 1 Thessalonians 4:11 (NLT) says: "Make it your goal to live a quiet life, minding your own business and working with your hands." We don't need to prove ourselves with our words. A quiet life while working with our hands is a great way to protect our peace and to stay out of trouble.

Proverbs 10:19 (NLT) says: "Too much talk leads to sin. Be sensible and keep your mouth shut." That verse sounds a little harsh, but our peace is worth far more than saying what we feel like we ought to say. It's much better and more peaceful to keep our lips sealed if what we are about to say will interrupt our peace. You could even silently say to yourself, "protect my peace," rather than responding with something that could bring something other than peace.

Romans 12:18 (NLT) says: "Do all that you can to live in peace with everyone."

God is not a God of confusion, and the devil wants more than anything for us to live in chaos, fear, and anxiety. God has given us a wide range of emotions to teach us things, but most importantly, He has given us the fruit of His spirit, which is love, joy, *peace*, patience, kindness, goodness, faithfulness, gentleness, and self-control. Psalm 121:1–2 (NIV) says: "I lift up my eyes to the mountains—where does my help come from? My help comes from the Lord, the Maker of Heaven and earth."

I could have allowed the enemy to ruin my wedding day by reminding me that I didn't have a dad to walk me down the aisle. I conquered that thought by envisioning my heavenly Father walking me down the aisle that day. He has been a good Father through all the joys and all the trials. He has given me guidance, support, love, comfort, forgiveness, and grace. I will follow my heavenly Father all the days of my life.

A lot of times we are not living in peace simply because we need to reframe our thoughts with what aligns with God's word and His truth. Reading God's word daily is a great routine to stay in God's comfort and to protect our peace. Social media has caused self-image, comparison, and acceptance to become obsessions and idols in the lives of many people. Social media is a great tool and resource to stay connected with family and friends, but if it is becoming a root cause of anxiety and depression, then that is an indicator to protect your peace by limiting your exposure to those platforms.

We must also protect our peace by guarding our eyes with what we see and what others see when they look at us. 1 Timothy 2:9 (NLT) says: "I want women to be modest in their appearance. They should wear decent and appropriate clothing and not draw attention to themselves by the way they fix their hair or by wearing gold or pearls or expensive clothes." Lust and envy will cause destruction, and we have the control to protect our peace by choosing what we allow our eyes to see and how we choose to visually present ourselves to others. James 1:14–15 (NLT) says: "Temptation comes from our own desires, which entice us and drag us away. These desires give birth to sinful actions. And when sin is allowed to grow, it gives birth to death."

1 Peter 3:4 (NIV) says: "Rather, it should be that of your inner self, the unfading beauty of a gentle and quiet spirit, which is of great worth in God's sight."

Chapter 19

YOUR MINISTRY

*W*e all have a ministry, and our greatest ministry will come from our deepest hurts. We know this to be true because 2 Timothy 4:5 (NLT) says: "Don't be afraid of suffering for the Lord. Work at telling others the Good News, and fully carry out the *ministry* God has given *you*."

This means that what you've gone through is equipping you to deliver someone else who will go through the same thing. God will use our painful experiences to groom us and prepare us for ministry. 2 Corinthians 1:4 (CSB) says: "He comforts us in all our affliction, so that we may be able to comfort those who are in any kind of affliction, through the comfort we ourselves receive from God."

Your assignment is to share your testimony with others. That's one of the many ways you can minister to others. Your testimony is the Good News of how you accepted Jesus, your life lessons, and how Christ has made a difference in your life. God wants us to share our life message with others. We must continue what Jesus started on this earth, and it is our mission to introduce people to God. Our mission is mandatory as Matthew 28:19 (NLT) tells us: "Go and make disciples of all the nations, baptizing them in the name of the Father and the Son and the Holy Spirit."

Our testimonies are more effective than sermons because testimonies are easier for people to relate to. Our stories capture people's attention, and our testimony will bypass any intellectual defenses or debates about the Bible. Within every hardship is a testimony, and we are here to share the goodness of God and to give other people hope on their journeys. When we are vulnerable, it creates a safe place for others to be vulnerable, too. Psalm 9:1 (NLT) says: "I will praise you, Lord, with all my heart; I will tell of all the marvelous things you have done."

God holds us accountable for the unbelievers on our path. We are the only Christians that some people will ever know and we are the only Bible that some people will ever read. God wants us to share the Good News with where we are, where God has planted us, and with the people around us that are on our journey. Who has God put on your path to tell about Jesus? You can simply tell them about what God has taught you and what you've learned by having a relationship with Jesus.

Are we using God for our purpose, or are we allowing God to use us for *His* purpose? Rather than having a presumptuous posture of demanding to know why things happen as they do, it's much better to ask God, "How do you want me to view this situation?" or "What do you want me to do right now?" Ask yourself, "How can my situation bring someone closer to Jesus?"

Everything great that God is going to do in your life, He's going to do through relationships and the gifts He planted inside us. God gave us all spiritual gifts to edify each other and to lift each other up. Ephesians 4:8 (NLT) says: "When Jesus ascended, He led a crowd of captives and gave *gifts* to His people." Ephesians 4:11 (NLT) clarifies what the gifts are: "These are the gifts Christ gave to the church: the apostles, the prophets, the evangelists, and the pastors and teachers. Their responsibility is to equip God's people to do His work and build up the church, the body of Christ. This will continue until we all come to such unity in our faith and knowledge of God's Son that we will be mature in the Lord, measuring up to the full and complete standard of Christ."

1 Corinthians 1:7 (NIV) tells us: "You do not lack any spiritual gifts as you eagerly wait for our Lord Jesus Christ to be revealed." 1 Corinthians 12:4 (NIV) says: "There are different kinds of gifts, but the same Spirit distributes them all." We all have gifts, and God wants us to use our gifts to point people to Him!

Whatever your gifts are, you will know if you are functioning in your gifts because you will have peace and joy. The anointing of God turns you into another person. 1 John 2:27 (NIV) says: "As for you, the anointing you received from Him remains in you, and you do not need anyone to teach you."

We cannot peacefully do what God has *not* anointed us to do, and we shouldn't try to live on the other side of our gifts. God gave us gifts so He can work through us and show His love to others through our earthy vessels. What we are doing should not be hard for us if God has anointed us to do it, and we shouldn't be miserable at what we are doing. If we are feeling miserable, then that is an indicator that we are not working within our spiritual gifts. God will enable us to do what we should do by giving us His wisdom and ease.

Chapter 20

REPORT FOR DUTY

So often we pray by bringing our requests to God, which is a wonderful thing to do by trusting the Lord with our needs. However, this last chapter is to inspire you and to teach you how to "report for duty" and to wake up every morning saying, "Dear Lord, I am here, use me today in a mighty way; I am available!"

Just like love and marriage, we don't just fall in love, we commit to the covenant. Love is saying, "I will be there no matter what." How can we tell God that we love Him, and that we'll be there for Him no matter what? By reporting each day for duty.

John 21:15 (NLT) says: "After breakfast, Jesus asked Simon Peter, "Simon, son of John, do you love me more than these?" "Yes, Lord," Peter replied, "you know I love you." "Then feed my lambs," Jesus told him."

Christ is saying in that verse that if we love Him, then we will serve others. He has equipped us with spiritual gifts to be able to serve people well. We can report for duty by searching for ways we can be the hand of God to someone. Proverbs 3:27 (NLT) says: "Do not withhold good from those who deserve it when it's in your power to help them." Matthew 10:42 (ESV) tells us: "And whoever gives one of these little ones even a cup of cold water because he is a disciple, truly, I say to you, he will by no means lose his reward."

The Bible tells us to also give cheerfully. 2 Corinthians 9 7–8 (NIV) says: "Each of you should give what you have decided in your heart to give, not reluctantly or under compulsion, for God loves a cheerful giver. And God can bless you abundantly, so that in all things at all times, having all that you need, you will abound in every good work."

The Lord wants us to cheerfully give our time, effort, energy, resources, talents, financial blessings, and gifts to point others to Christ. We must continuously ask Him to fill up our cups so we can pour into others. Matthew 10:39 (NLT) says: "If you cling to your life, you will lose it; but if you give up your life for me, you will find it."

Acts 20:24 (NLT) says: "But my life is worth nothing to me unless I use it for finishing the work assigned me by the Lord Jesus—the work of telling others the Good News about the wonderful grace of God."

May you find joy in serving the Lord and may
your testimony bring others to Christ Jesus.

"If you declare with your mouth, 'Jesus
is Lord,' and believe in your heart that
God raised Jesus from the dead, you
will be saved" (Romans 10:9 NIV)

I believe that Jesus Christ is the Son of the Living God,
and I want Him to be the Lord of my life. I want God to
take my life and use it for His glory. I am His vessel to
shine His light and to share the Good News with others.

_____

Signed

_____

Date

If this book led you to accept Jesus
and to become a Christian, hallelujah!
Praise God! There is rejoicing in Heaven
for you right now! (Luke 15:7 NIV)

Now that you have accepted Jesus, here are
some helpful things to consider next:

1. Begin to read the Bible. The Bible is God's
instruction book on how to live your life in a way
that pleases Him. God's word is our weapon against
the enemy, and there are so many remarkable
stories and parables in the Bible, too! Our life
mission is to learn how to become like Jesus!

2. Find a church home. This will become a place
you will learn about God and meet other believers.
The church was God's idea, and He has equipped
pastors with spiritual gifts to teach us and to watch
over our souls just like a shepherd watches over his
sheep. The church will become a wonderful place
you can serve and use your spiritual gifts, too!

3. Pray. Praying simply means talking to
God. God wants us to bring Him our requests,
petitions, and praises. God wants us to talk to
Him on our good days and our bad days.

4. Consider being baptized. Jesus was baptized by his
cousin, John the Baptist. We are "born again" when

we are baptized and made new by the cleansing and washing away of our old selves. This is an especially crucial step in your growth with Jesus. It is also how you let people know that you have decided to follow Jesus. Acts 2:38 (NLT) says: "Each of you must repent of your sins and turn to God and be baptized in the name of Jesus Christ for the forgiveness of your sins. Then you will receive the gift of the Holy Spirit."

Behold what manner of love the
Father has given to us, that we
should be called children of God.

—1 John 3:1 (BSB)

Always be prepared to give an answer
to everyone who asks you to give the
reason for the hope that you have.

—1 Peter 3:15 (NIV)

Use the next blank page to write out your story.

Here are some helpful tips to help you
write out your testimony:

1. Your life before you accepted Jesus.

2. Why you needed Jesus.

3. Your commitment to Jesus.

4. The difference Jesus has made in your life.

Your testimony is the best way to help lead others
to Jesus. Your personal story is more effective
than quoting the Bible to people because no
one can ever argue with your testimony.

Your Testimony

STUDY GUIDE/GROUP DISCUSSION

The next section of this book was created to guide you with self-reflection, journaling, or group discussions. Each page will give you thought-provoking questions related to the chapters of this book. Prayer, journaling, and deep conversations are great ways to bring clarity and healing to our thoughts and feelings.

CHAPTER 1: ON THE MOUNTAINTOP

I have come that they may have
life and have it to the full.

—John 10:10 (NIV)

1. Describe your upbringing and any challenges you may have had growing up.

2. Looking back, can you identify times in your childhood when God had His hand of protection over you?

3. What was your life like before you accepted Jesus?

4. Was there a time in your life that you were too busy for God?

5. What would you tell your younger self?

CHAPTER 2: IN THE VALLEY

The Lord himself goes before you and will be
with you; He will never leave you nor forsake
you. Do not be afraid; do not be discouraged.

—Deuteronomy 31:8 (NIV)

1. Do you remember the first time you truly prayed to God?
   If so, what was that experience like?

2. What was the first trial or tragedy you experienced?

3. Who are some people that have been there for you during
   your trying times? Who did you want to be there?

4. Do you recall some of the first Bible scriptures that spoke
   to you and if so, which ones were they?

5. Have you lost a loved one to death? How did it make you
   feel?

CHAPTER 3: A NEW NORMAL

Cast all your anxiety on Him
because He cares for you.

—1 Peter 5:7 (NIV)

1. What was the hardest funeral you attended? Who was there? How did that experience make you feel?

2. How did you mourn?

3. What type of questions did you have during that time? Do you still have those questions?

4. What gave you comfort? What brought you joy during those days?

5. In what ways did you grow through your grief? What did your grief teach you?

CHAPTER 4: WHY IS THIS HAPPENING?

I have made you and I will carry you. I
will sustain you and I will rescue you.

—Isaiah 46:4 (NIV)

1. Was there ever a time in your life that you thought God was the reason for the tribulations you were enduring?

2. In what ways did God bring goodness from the trial you went through?

3. Are there any situations in your life that you can look back on with a clearer perspective?

4. Who are some people in your life that you can pray for that you typically don't pray for?

5. In what ways have you been blessed after persevering under trial?

CHAPTER 5: HEAVENLY VS. WORLDLY

Cling to what is good.

—Romans 12:9 (NIV)

1. What are some things in your life that you can surrender to ensure God is number one?

2. What are some things you can do today that will impact Heaven?

3. Is there heavenly wisdom that you're thankful you learned after enduring struggles?

4. What is something that you typically tend to worry about that you want to surrender?

5. Can you share some examples of how the Lord has been there for you through any hard times?

CHAPTER 6: TRIGGERS

Keep me safe, my God, for
in You I take refuge.

—Psalm 16:1 (NIV)

1. What are some things that trigger you?

2. What are some ways you can slow down your response to those triggers?

3. Do you have some reoccurring thoughts that you can work on reframing?

4. What is a scripture that you can memorize to speak aloud?

5. What are some ways you can be proactive and plan if you know a trigger may be approaching?

CHAPTER 7: MOVING FORWARD

Be strong and courageous! Do not be
afraid or discouraged. For the Lord, your
God is with you wherever you go.

—Joshua 1:9 (NLT)

1. Is there someone in your life that you need to forgive to move forward?

2. Is there forgiveness from the Lord that you need to receive?

3. What are some things that inspire you to take steps forward?

4. Is there someone or something that you have up on a pedestal that needs to be removed?

5. What fills your soul?

CHAPTER 8: EMBRACING LIFE

At the right time, I, the Lord,
will make it happen.

—Isaiah 60:22 (NLT)

1. Can you name and acknowledge some earthly angels you've had on your journey?

2. Have you had some seasons in your life where you had to really focus on your obedience to the Lord?

3. How is the Lord currently using you in a mighty way?

4. What are some things you've experienced in your life that groomed you for something bigger?

5. Have you gone through some suffering and the Lord later revealed something greater?

CHAPTER 9: CLOUD NINE

His love endures forever.

—Psalm 118:1 (NIV)

1. Can you name a time that the Lord miraculously moved in your life?

2. What was the biggest change you've gone through?

3. When in your life have you been on cloud nine?

4. What was the best day of your life?

5. How can you continue living out your best day?

CHAPTER 10: DEEP WATERS

He calmed the storm to a whisper
and stilled the waves.

—Psalm 107:29 (NLT)

1. Have you gone through something beautiful that led you into some deep waters?

2. Who in your life have you seen God work through to be there for you?

3. What are some positive emotions that you want to magnify?

4. What are some ways you can pay a tribute to things you've suffered?

5. What are some things that you're thankful for right now?

CHAPTER 11: PEOPLE PLEASING

You will show me the way of life, granting
me the joy of Your presence and the
pleasures of living with You forever.

—Psalm 16:11 (NLT)

1. Are there people in your life that you strive to please?

2. What are some ways that you can please God before others?

3. What do you do daily that pleases the Lord?

4. Are there people in your life that depend on your affirmation or approval?

5. How can you help others live for God's approval before your approval?

CHAPTER 12: URGENCY

Jesus often withdrew to lonely
places and prayed.

—Luke 5:16 (NIV)

1. What are some ways that you can have more childlike faith?

2. Do you feel as though you urgently run to the Lord in your time of need?

3. Is God the first one you thank when your prayers are answered?

4. What are some ways that you can have better conversations with God?

5. How can you find ways to urgently run to your heavenly Father more?

CHAPTER 13: SUFFERING WELL

For though I fall, I will rise again.

—Micah 7:8 (NLT)

1. Has there been a time in your life when you've cried out to God?

2. Have you experienced a painful situation that made you better instead of bitter?

3. Are there ways you can focus on the purpose of some of the pain you've gone through?

4. Have you grown closer to people through your weaknesses?

5. Who in your life have you been honored to struggle alongside?

CHAPTER 14: THE POWER OF WORDS

Gentle words are a tree of life; a
deceitful tongue crushes the spirit.

—Proverbs 15:4 (NLT)

1. What are some things you could start saying to bless others?

2. How can you ask for God's help to tame your tongue?

3. Have there been some words you've said that you've regretted?

4. Has there been a time in your life where your words interfered with God's blessings?

5. Are there situations in your life where you can remain quieter?

CHAPTER 15: CHOOSING JOY

Be joyful in hope, patient in
affliction, and faithful in prayer.

—Romans 12:12 (NIV)

1. Are you receiving the gift of joy that the Lord has available to you?

2. Are there some things you can forgive to have more access to your joy?

3. What are some ways you can stay joyful through your challenges?

4. Are there things you're comparing your life to that is stealing your joy?

5. What are some things that you can say aloud to rebuke the enemy and remain more joyful?

CHAPTER 16: THE WAITING

This is the day the Lord has made.
We will rejoice and be glad in it."

—Psalm 118:24 (NLT)

1. Have you gone through a waiting season when you've waited for the next door in your life to open?

2. What was your waiting season like?

3. What did you learn during your waiting season?

4. Did you remain steadfast in prayer through your waiting season?

5. What were some blessings around you that you noticed while you were waiting for the next chapter to begin?

CHAPTER 17: IS SATAN OUT TO GET ME?

Counsel and sound judgment are
mine; I have insight, I have power.

—Proverbs 8:14 (NIV)

1. In what ways have you felt under attack by the enemy?

2. What are ways that you fight back when Satan is after you?

3. How do you know if it's the enemy that's challenging you?

4. How can you inspire others to rebuke the devil?

5. What verses can you begin speaking aloud when you're under attack?

CHAPTER 18: PROTECT YOUR PEACE

You keep him in perfect peace whose mind
is stayed on You because he trusts in You.

—Isaiah 26:3 (ESV)

1. When do you feel the most peaceful?

2. What are new ways that you can embrace daily peace?

3. Who are the people in your life that bring you the most peace?

4. How can you reframe negative thoughts to embrace more peace?

5. How can you begin protecting your peace going forward?

CHAPTER 19: YOUR MINISTRY

I urge you to live a life worthy of the
calling you have received. Be completely
humble and gentle; be patient,
bearing with one another in love.

—Ephesians 4:1–2 (NIV)

1. What is the most profound pain you've gone through?

2. How can you use your painful experiences to minister to others?

3. How can you begin to share your testimony more often?

4. What are your spiritual gifts?

5. How can you use your gifts to point others to Christ?

CHAPTER 20: REPORT FOR DUTY

Those who sow with tears will
reap with songs of joy.

—Psalm 126:5 (NIV)

1. How do you usually pray? When do you pray?

2. What are some new ways you can pray or make prayer a priority?

3. How do you want the Lord to use you?

4. How can we serve others more to show Christ that we love Him?

5. Where has the Lord placed you to fulfill the assignment that He's given you?

Printed in the United States
by Baker & Taylor Publisher Services